100
A CENTURY OF NHL MEMORIES

Phil Pritchard with Jim Hynes
Foreword by Lanny McDonald

Rare Photos from the Hockey Hall of Fame

A Century of NHL Memories - *Rare Photos from the Hockey Hall of Fame*
Phil Pritchard with Jim Hynes

Content Curation
Griffintown Media in Partnership with the Hockey Hall of Fame

Published in Canada by Griffintown Media Inc.
5548 Saint-Patrick Street, Montreal, QC H4E 1A9
(514) 934-2474 | info@griffintown.com | griffintown.com

All photos were provided from the collections of the Hockey Hall of Fame

ISBN 978-0-9958630-0-2

Printed in Canada by Friesens (Manitoba)

PRODUCTION CREDITS

Content Curation

The Hockey Hall of Fame
Phil Pritchard
Craig Campbell
Steve Poirier

Griffintown Media
Salma Belhaffaf
Jim Hynes
Jim McRae

Concept, Design & Production

Griffintown Media
Jim McRae, President
Salma Belhaffaf, Senior Designer
Katrysha Gellis, Project Coordinator
Anne Nice, Editorial Assistant
Judy Yelon, Proofreader
Valerie Woods, Book Web Site Developer

To the photographers who captured these amazing memories.

Montreal Forum · Montreal, QC | 1964-65 ◯ Frank Prazak | colour · transparency · 2¼" x 2¼"

TABLE OF Contents

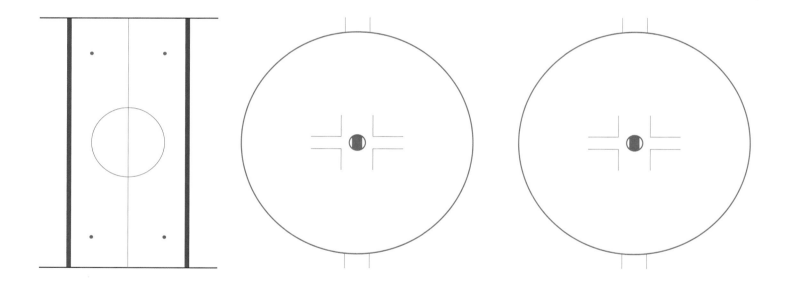

LANNY McDONALD

HHOF 1992

I'm one of the biggest fans hockey could possibly have. Perhaps it's only fitting — actually it's a blessing — that my "second" career in the game is as Chairman of the Board for the Hockey Hall of Fame. It provides me with the opportunity to travel the country and meet the best people you can imagine in and around the sport. It reminds me that even though we celebrate milestones like the NHL's 100th anniversary, the game hasn't really changed much at its core. It's all about people and passion, which best summarizes my role at the Hall.

One of the questions I'm asked most when I visit with people at games and community events, after the moustache question — I've had it since 1974, my second year in the league — is what is my fondest memory from my career? It was the first time I walked into Maple Leaf Gardens as a rookie. It was dark with the only light shining in from the outdoors through the exits. It was eerie in a way, but also a dream come true and something I'll always remember. That's something that's obviously very personal to me, but when I look through the photos on the following pages, I can't help but think that so many of the images will bring back memories of their own for readers. I'm excited to see shots of players who I looked up to before joining the NHL, like Gordie Howe and Jean Béliveau, players who I dreamed I could become just a little bit like one day.

It also gives me great pride to note that all of the photos in the book are from the Hall's photo archives, which really means that they come from the men and women who generously donated them to our collection. Actually, they entrusted us with them, which is an enormous responsibility we take very seriously. More than just caretakers, we are the custodians of memories, and memories are the ties to generations, especially in our sport where history is celebrated like in no other. Over the years, our archives have grown to more than three million images, becoming one of the largest hockey photo collections in the world. That's the ultimate compliment to the team at our D.K. (Doc) Seaman Hockey Resource Centre, and the ultimate sign of trust from our donors.

It's often been written about me that I was fortunate to end my career on the highest note, winning the Stanley Cup in my final game. I was also lucky enough to score that night, but my biggest memories were of the respect the Montreal fans showed us as my Calgary teammates and I skated around with the Cup on Forum ice. They stood and applauded even though their team had lost. I also thought it was the most peaceful feeling you could ever imagine even with all the excitement going on around me. The photo (page 132) brings back that game like it was yesterday. It's a memory I'll keep forever.

INTRODUCTION

Hockey fans will be more familiar with its wonderful displays in the former Bank of Montreal building in downtown Toronto, but the Hockey Hall of Fame is much more than a museum. Since it was first established in 1943, the Hall has been collecting all manner of historical items and hockey-related material dating from the turn of the 20th century to today, not the least of which is its incredible photographic collection. Housed together with its vast archive of publications and other printed materials, as well as personal collections, the Hall's collection of photos has resided in the D.K. (Doc) Seaman Resource Centre within the MasterCard Centre for Hockey Excellence since 2009. It contains more than half a million digitized photos and its cold room preserves more than two million negatives and slides, 750 glass negatives, and 32,000 printed photos, the vast majority of which have never been published — which brings us to the idea behind this book.

A Century of NHL Memories celebrates the NHL's centennial by throwing open the doors to the Hall of Fame's archives and unveiling some of the photographic collection's hidden treasures. Often snapped by legends of photojournalism, and selected from the Hall of Fame's collection for their beauty and originality, or both, these 130 photos cast hockey's heroes in a different light, take you into the heart of the action, as fierce as that may be, and bring you behind the scenes, often to a more innocent time in NHL history. Some will teach you something you didn't already know. Others will make you laugh.

In selecting these photos, we put special emphasis on originality. Hockey books tend to show the same shots over and over again, often with good reason. But with so many wonderful images at our disposal, we wanted to bring you something, if not quite new, then certainly different, including choosing to run many of the photos with minimal corrections so as to convey the time-capsule feel they offer; framing, scratches, notations on the images and, in some cases, uneven sight lines in action shots are all intentional. We're reasonably sure this approach will appeal to both lovers of the game and of great photography.

That said, we couldn't resist sprinkling in a handful of classics here and there. And when we could, we offered a different perspective, as in the case of what is arguably the greatest hockey photo ever, that of Bobby Orr, taken by Ray Lussier on May 10, 1970, flying through the air after having just scored the Stanley Cup-winning goal. That moment is captured here, but by two other photographers who took their own shots a fraction of a second earlier from different parts of the rink.

Looking through the Hockey Hall of Fame's photographic collection was a dream come true for the hockey fans that put together *A Century of NHL Memories*, a rare privilege indeed. We hope you enjoy them as much as we enjoyed bringing them to you.

Montreal Forum · Montreal, QC | January 1959   Studio Alain Brouillard | B/W · negative · 4" x 5"

William Osser Xavier "Bill" Cook was the first player signed by the New York Rangers on their entrance to the NHL in 1926 as well as the team's first captain, thus earning him the title "The Original Ranger." Playing right wing on the prolific "Bread Line" with his brother "Bun" and centreman Frank Boucher, Cook went on to lead the NHL in goals (33) and points (37) that inaugural season and helped the team to Stanley Cup titles in 1928 and 1933.

Bill Cook

HHOF 1952

OUR HEROES

They come in different shapes and sizes, from different eras, and even different countries, displaying different skill sets, and enthralling fans in different cities, be it with their breathtaking ability, sheer determination, raw power or a combination thereof. These are hockey's heroes, the players that inspired us from childhood: They are the legends of the game, the foundation upon which it was built, the larger-than-life figures that captured our collective imagination…and gripped it firmly. From the NHL's first stars to future Hall-of-Famers, see them here, sometimes lost in the moment, in deep concentration, or perhaps cast in a different light.

Of course, the NHL has brought us many more heroes than those featured on the pages that follow. These photos were selected to represent a variety of players, teams, styles and eras. But, perhaps more importantly, they were chosen for what they and their subjects shared: greatness.

What does Francis "King" Clancy, born in Ottawa, Ont., in 1903, have in common with Patrik Laine, born in Tampere, Finland, some 95 years later? What links Pavel Bure, who won the Calder Trophy with the Vancouver Canucks in 1992, with Chicago's Jonathan Toews, who scored 24 goals in his rookie season a decade-and-a-half later? It's a passion for the game, perhaps best described as a certain look in their eyes that shines through in these often rare shots, whether they were taken with a heavy Graflex camera favoured by early news photographers or a state-of-the-art digital single-lens reflex camera with a 400mm objective lens, in the heat of battle, formally posed or simply caught unawares.

Remembering Our Heroes.

Is it any wonder that Bobby Hull was the "rock star" of his generation? The speed, strength, good looks — and that hair — all combined to ensure all eyes were on "The Golden Jet" whenever he touched the puck, including in this wonderful photo of him powering up from behind the net.

Bobby Hull

HHOF 1983

Madison Square Garden · New York, NY | 1963-64 ◇ Harold Barkley | colour · transparency · 2³/₄" x 4¹/₂"

Mario Lemieux splits Rich Pilon and Jeff Norton before beating goaltender Kelly Hrudey in a 5-3 Pittsburgh defeat of the New York Islanders on December 20, 1988. The play was immortalized in a 10-foot, 4,700-pound bronze statue called "Le Magnifique" that was unveiled in March 2012 outside the then Consol Energy Center, across the street from the old Pittsburgh "Igloo."

Mario Lemieux

HHOF 1997

Civic Arena · Pittsburgh, PA | December 20, 1988 ⃟ Paul Bereswill | colour · slide · 35mm

Maple Leaf Gardens · Toronto, ON | 1954-55   Michael Burns Sr. | B/W · negative · 4" x 5"

The "Rocket" never took it easy. His opponents employed all manner of tactics, legal and otherwise, to slow him down, but from 1942 to 1960, through injury and fatigue, he played every one of his NHL shifts at top speed.

Maurice Richard

HHOF 1961

A rugged defenceman for nine NHL seasons, John Brian Patrick "Pat" Quinn looked and sounded for all the world like a stereotypical tough Irish cop. And those characteristics would serve "The Big Irishman," as he was known, very well in a legendary coaching career that lasted exactly 1,400 games. Quinn, who did double-duty as coach and GM in both Vancouver and Toronto, won an Olympic gold medal as the coach of Team Canada in 2002.

Pat Quinn

HHOF 2016

Although his name today is synonymous with the Maple Leafs, Francis Michael "King" Clancy played 10 seasons with his hometown Ottawa Senators before joining Toronto via a trade in 1930. A scoring defenceman acknowledged as one of the finest to ever play the game, Clancy incredibly worked as an NHL referee for 11 seasons following his playing career before moving on to coach the Maple Leafs for three years. The King Clancy Memorial Trophy for leadership qualities was created in his honour.

King Clancy

HHOF 1958

Location Unknown | Undated ⃟ Imperial Oil – Turofsky | B/W · glass · 4" x 5"

There was nothing like witnessing "The Russian Rocket" in flight. Pavel Bure used his trademark blazing speed to score 34 goals and win the Calder Trophy as Rookie-of-the-Year in 1992 and followed that up with two consecutive 60-goal seasons. After a trade sent him to the Florida Panthers in 1998, Bure enjoyed seasons of 58 and 59 goals in 1999-2000 and 2000-01. He retired at age 32 in 2003 due to chronic knee injuries.

Pavel Bure

HHOF 2012

Pacific Coliseum · Vancouver, BC | 1991-92 ⬦ Chris Relke | colour · negative · 35mm

Jonathan Toews eludes a stick check from Edmonton's
Sam Gagner. The man Chicago Blackhawks fans have
dubbed "Captain Serious" is among the NHL's most respected
players. The bilingual Winnipeg native has helped lead the
Blackhawks to three Stanley Cup championships since
being named team captain in 2008-09 and was a key part
of two Olympic gold-medal-winning teams for Canada.

Jonathan Toews

You could argue that no one has been in more Canadian hockey rinks than Cochrane, Ontario-native Myles "Tim" Horton, first as a player for 22 NHL seasons and then as the namesake of the coffee and snack food of choice for hockey players and their families. A defenceman renowned for his physical strength and considerable offensive skill, Horton played 18 full seasons for the Toronto Maple Leafs, winning four Stanley Cup championships. He opened the first Tim Hortons donut shop, in Hamilton, Ontario, in 1964. Horton passed away in a tragic car accident while playing for the Buffalo Sabres in 1974. He was 44.

Tim Horton

HHOF 1977

St. Louis Arena · St. Louis, MO | October 21, 1972　◯　Portnoy | colour · slide · 35mm

A native of Fredericton, New Brunswick, Boston Bruins winger Willie O'Ree became the first black player to take part in an NHL game on January 18, 1958, in Montreal. O'Ree, who had lost most of the vision in his right eye in a minor-league game two years earlier, played again in a Canadiens-Bruins rematch the following night. He then bounced around the minor leagues for two more years before finally playing 43 more NHL games for Boston in 1960-61.

Willie O'Ree

Maple Leaf Gardens · Toronto, ON | 1960-61   Imperial Oil-Turofsky | B/W · negative · 4" x 5"

The pride of Cole Harbour, Nova Scotia, Sidney Crosby became the youngest captain in NHL history when he succeeded Mario Lemieux in that role in 2007-08. Well on his way to being one of the most decorated players in the game, "Sid the Kid" had precociously captured three Stanley Cup championships, two Conn Smythe trophies as playoff MVP and numerous other awards — all before the age of 30.

Sidney Crosby

BB&T Center · Sunrise, FL | December 22, 2014   Ward Benjamin | colour · digital

It didn't take long for the Vancouver Canucks to regret trading the player they chose in the first round, ninth overall of the 1983 NHL Entry Draft to the Boston Bruins in 1986. In his first season with the Bruins, the 6'1", 220-lb native of Comox, B.C., scored 36 goals on his way to becoming one of the greatest power forwards of his time. In 1992, playing in only 49 games due to one of the injuries that would plague his career, Neely scored a remarkable 50 goals.

Cam Neely

HHOF 2005

"Killer" is a bit of an odd nickname for a player who confessed to weighing only 175 pounds "soaking wet." Kingston, Ontario, native Doug Gilmour was given his deadly moniker by St. Louis Blues teammate Brian Sutter for his apparent resemblance to one notorious murderer and his surname being similar to that of another. Gilmour's skill, passion, fearlessness and gritty determination made him one of the best players in hockey. In 1992-93 and 1993-94, he led the Toronto Maple Leafs in scoring and on long playoff runs with seasons of 127 and 111 points respectively. He retired in 2003 with 450 goals and 964 assists.

Doug Gilmour

HHOF 2011

Maple Leaf Gardens · Toronto, ON | April 25, 1993 ◯ Doug MacLellan | colour · slide · 35mm

You would think that the player who owns the NHL's record book also possessed the best tools in the game — speed, strength, size. He didn't. What set Wayne Gretzky apart from all others, however, was his vision and imagination. This poignant shot of "The Great One" shows him getting ready to enter the fray, already strategizing his next improbable move.

Wayne Gretzky

HHOF 1999

Brendan Byrne Arena · Meadowlands, NJ | January 15, 1984 ○ Paul Bereswill | colour · slide · 35mm

The old and the new: Chicago veteran Marián Hossa staves off a
check from Winnipeg rookie sensation Patrik Laine during the 2016-17
NHL season. Laine, a native of Tampere, Finland, and the second-overall
pick in the 2016 NHL Entry Draft, would go on to score 36 goals in his
debut campaign. Hossa, the Slovakian star who played his first game in
1997, scored his 500th NHL goal in the fourth game of the season.

Patrik Laine & Marián Hossa

MTS Centre · Winnipeg, MB | November 15, 2016 ◯ Rusty Barton | colour · digital

CLASSIC PHOTOS

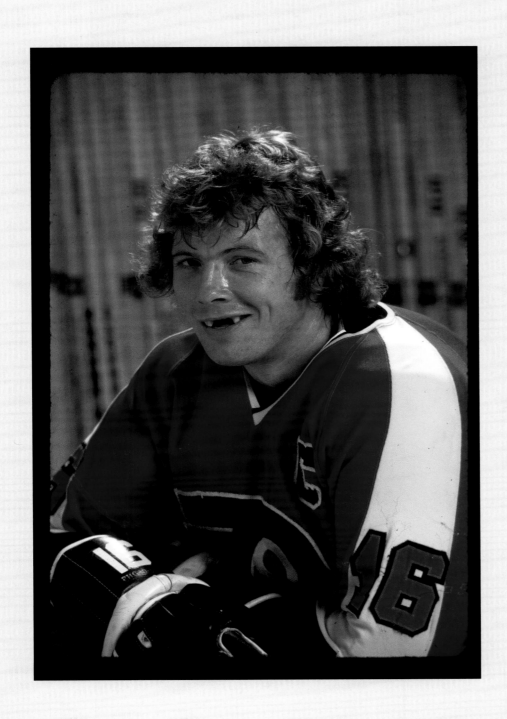

For all his success as one of hockey's ultimate — and gritty — leaders, Philadelphia Flyers' famous captain Bobby Clarke might be best remembered for his toothless "hockey" smile, captured here in this classic shot.

Bobby Clarke

⚜ HHOF 1987 ⚜

Location Unknown | September 1973   John Hanlon | colour · slide · 35mm

California Golden Seals goalie Gary Smith uses the paddle of his stick to block the puck. The Ottawa native, who played Junior Hockey with the Toronto St. Michael's Majors and Marlboros, actually made his NHL debut with the Maple Leafs in 1965-66 before being claimed by the California franchise in the 1967 draft. Smith, who played 532 games for seven different franchises, surrendered the last goal in the history of the World Hockey Association, on May 20, 1979, to Edmonton's Dave Semenko while playing for the Winnipeg Jets.

Gary Smith

Maple Leaf Gardens · Toronto, ON | 1970-71 ⏀ Graphic Artists | colour · transparency · 2¼" x 2¼"

GOALTENDERS

They are often hockey's most eccentric players, sometimes intense, often quirky, almost always interesting. And no wonder. Goalies, by virtue of their job description and equipment alone, stand out in a hockey team's lineup. But in nature and personality, the guardians of the goal are, well, different, too. Some are grim and determined. Others are more easygoing, using humour to diminish and cope with the extraordinary level of stress that inevitably comes with their dangerous and unique vocation. Lots of them are nervous wrecks, while others are the game's sharpest students. Whatever category individual hockey goaltenders fall into, these characters make for the most intriguing subjects to photograph in all of sport.

In the pre-mask days, the goalies' expressions were laid bare for all to see. Fear, intense concentration, vulnerability, anger, joy... all could be observed on their unprotected faces. With the birth of the mask in 1959, those emotions would become more difficult to read, yet this would only add to the goalie mystique, especially with the advent of mask art, and later, colourful and beautifully designed pads and gloves. Combining their personalized gear with their grace and athleticism made goalies even cooler.

The photographs selected here span some 80 years, and feature some of goaltending's greatest. Most are Hall-of-Famers, like the wonderfully monikered Walter "Turk" Broda and Rogatien "Rogie" Vachon, the former inducted in 1967, the latter of the Class of 2016. Some of them will surely be enshrined in the near future, while others are simply here because they happen to be the main focus of a great hockey photo.

Enjoy these great goalie memories.

New Jersey Devils goalie Martin Brodeur prepares to snag a shot
during the 2005-06 season. Arguably the most successful goaltender
of all time, Brodeur employed a hybrid stand-up/butterfly style
to great success. The Montreal native retired in 2015 owning NHL
records for all-time goaltender wins and shutouts. He led the Devils
to three Stanley Cup championships and was part of two Olympic
gold-medal-winners with Team Canada.

Martin Brodeur

Corel Centre · Kanata, ON | March 28, 2006 ◯ Dave Sandford | colour · digital

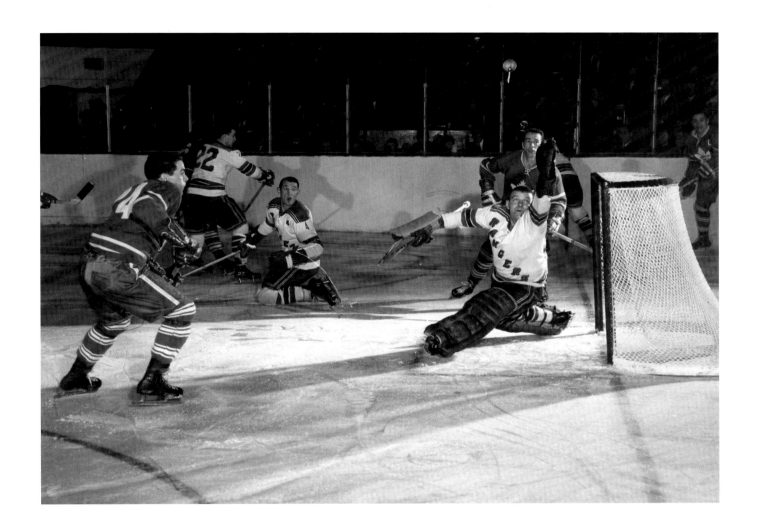

Lorne "Gump" Worsley of the New York Rangers makes a dramatic glove save against the Leafs. The Montreal native is said to have earned his nickname for his resemblance to Andy Gump, a character from the popular comic strip "The Gumps." Legend has it that Worsley once sustained a concussion after being hit in the head by a hard-boiled egg thrown by a fan in New York while playing for the visiting Canadiens. The second to last barefaced NHL goaltender, "Gumper" retired in 1974 having played 855 of his 861 career games without a mask.

Gump Worsley

HHOF 1980

A young Walter "Turk" Broda scrambles to make a save against the
Black Hawks. Note that both teams were wearing dark sweaters, with
contrasting colours not made mandatory by the NHL until 1950. The
Black Hawks won their second championship in 1938, defeating the
Leafs 3-1 in the Stanley Cup Final. Broda would go on to play 13 full
seasons with Toronto, winning five championships. He missed two
seasons while serving in the army during World War II.

Turk Broda

HHOF 1967

Chicago Stadium · Chicago, IL | 1938-39 ◯ Le Studio du Hockey | B/W · negative · 4" x 5"

Terry Sawchuk, the tortured legend of the Detroit Red Wings, keeps his eye on the prize in a game against the Maple Leafs. The Winnipeg native played in 971 games over 21 NHL seasons, from 1950 to 1970, acquiring a litany of gruesome injuries along the way. Sawchuk long held the league goaltending records in wins and shutouts. Unless the NHL drops the shootout one day, his one remaining record, 172 career ties, will never be broken. A four-time Stanley Cup champion, Sawchuk actually had three tours of duty with the Red Wings, the final one lasting only 13 games in 1968–69. He died in May 1970 at age 40.

Terry Sawchuk

HHOF 1971

Maple Leaf Gardens · Toronto, ON | January 6, 1960 ⊕ Imperial Oil-Turofsky | B/W · negative · 4" x 5"

Henrik Lundqvist of the New York Rangers stretches to make the save against Toronto. The native of Are, Sweden, went on to become the only goaltender in history to win 30 games in each of his first seven NHL seasons, and in 2017 became the fastest goaltender to reach the 400-win mark. Lundqvist led Sweden to a gold medal at the 2006 Olympics, a silver at the 2014 Games and gold at the 2017 IIHF World Championships.

Henrik Lundqvist

Air Canada Centre · Toronto, ON | October 21, 2006   Dave Sandford | colour · digital

Eddie Belfour slides across his crease to make a save against the Tampa Bay Lightning. In 1991, Belfour was the winner of both the Calder and Vezina trophies, and he won a second Vezina in 1993. Nicknamed "The Eagle," he spent parts of eight seasons in Chicago before stops in San Jose, Dallas, Toronto and Florida. Belfour won a Stanley Cup with the Stars in 1999. He is one of only two players to win an NCAA championship, an Olympic gold medal and a Stanley Cup.

Eddie Belfour

HHOF 2011

Expo Hall · Tampa, FL **|** 1992-93   Paul Bereswill **|** colour · slide · 35mm

Maple Leaf Gardens · Toronto, ON | November 4, 1961   Michael Burns Sr. | B/W · negative · 4" x 5"

Toronto Maple Leafs legend Johnny Bower goes airborne
to block a high shot. After 12 seasons in the minors, "The
China Wall" finally became a permanent NHLer in 1958,
when he was almost 34 years old. He led the Leafs to four
Stanley Cup championships, the last in 1967 at age 42, and
played his final game in December 1969 at age 45, making
him the oldest regular goalie ever to play an NHL game.
Bower was actually born John Kiszkan, in Prince Albert,
Saskatchewan. He changed his name in his first season
of pro hockey. Bower is also known to have lied about his
age at least twice, once to appear older to enlist in the
army, and then later to seem younger to NHL scouts.

Johnny Bower

HHOF 1976

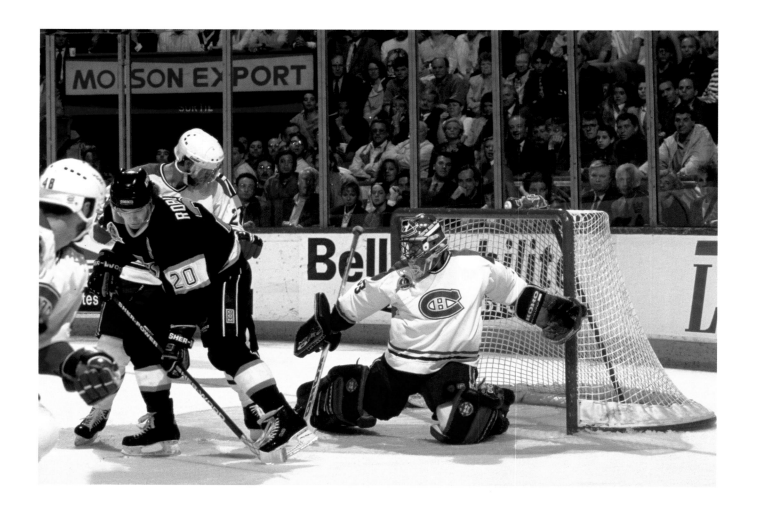

Patrick Roy employs the butterfly stance he made famous while defenceman Eric Desjardins ties up Luc Robitaille of the Los Angeles Kings. "St-Patrick" won two Stanley Cup championships with the Canadiens and two more with the Colorado Avalanche. The 1993 Cup conquest was the most memorable, however, as Roy held the fort during 10 consecutive Montreal overtime wins. The winner of three Conn Smythe trophies as playoff MVP, Roy holds the record for most playoff games (247) and wins (151) by a goaltender.

Patrick Roy

HHOF 2006

A high shot flies inches from the face of Glenn Hall of the Chicago Black Hawks as Toronto Maple Leafs captain and familiar foe George Armstrong looks on. Often credited with pioneering the butterfly style, "Mr. Goalie" played a record 502 consecutive games, all without a mask, over a span of eight seasons (including playoffs) and helped the Black Hawks end a 23-year Stanley Cup drought in 1961. Owner of one of sports' most legendarily nervous stomachs, Hall actually started his career with Detroit, where he was the NHL's Rookie-of-the-Year for 1955-56, and ended with the St. Louis Blues in 1971.

Glenn Hall

HHOF 1975

Maple Leaf Gardens · Toronto, ON | 1961–62 Imperial Oil - Turofsky | B/W · negative · 4" x 5"

NHL legend Joseph Jacques Omer Plante was an innovator throughout his career, including having introduced the goalie mask in 1959. The avid knitter is shown here battling with fellow future Hall-of-Famer Frank Mahovlich, while Jean-Guy Talbot is about to take exception.

Jacques Plante

HHOF 1978

Maple Leaf Gardens · Toronto, ON | December 30, 1959 ⟡ Harold Barkley | colour · transparency · 2¼" x 2¼"

Rogatien "Rogie" Vachon wasn't afraid to wander from his net even with the likes of Bobby Hull on his tail. The diminutive native of Palmarolle, Quebec was called up to Montreal in 1967 to replace the injured "Gump" Worsley, and ended up leading the team to the Stanley Cup Final against Toronto, where Leafs coach Punch Imlach famously referred to him as a "Junior 'B' goalie." The Leafs won that Cup but Vachon was a member of the Canadiens team that won the next two. Vachon was traded to Los Angeles in 1971. In 1976, he was the MVP of Team Canada, winning the Canada Cup. Vachon was the Kings' assistant then head coach in 1983-84, and general manager from 1984 to 1992. His number 30 was the first Kings jersey to be retired.

Rogie Vachon

HHOF 2016

New York Rangers Mike Richter goes through his pre-game stretching
routine. Known for his reflexes and acrobatic saves, the Abington,
Pennsylvania, native played his entire NHL career for the Rangers,
with whom he captured the Stanley Cup in 1994. A member of the
U.S. Hockey Hall of Fame, Richter represented his country in three
Olympic Games, the 1986 World Junior championships, the 1991
Canada Cup and the 1996 World Cup of Hockey.

Mike Richter

Nassau Veterans Memorial Coliseum · Uniondale, NY | Undated ○ Paul Bereswill | colour · slide · 35mm

The mask that started it all. A notorious joker, Gerry Cheevers of the Boston Bruins accidentally invented goalie mask art when he started adding stitch marks to his mask every time it got hit with a puck. The mask seen here is the first Cheevers ordered from Boston-based mask maker Ernie Higgins in the late 1960s. When young fans would ask how they too could have such a cool mask, the two-time Stanley Cup champ would reply, "Send me $100 and I'll send you a magic marker."

Gerry Cheevers

HHOF 1985

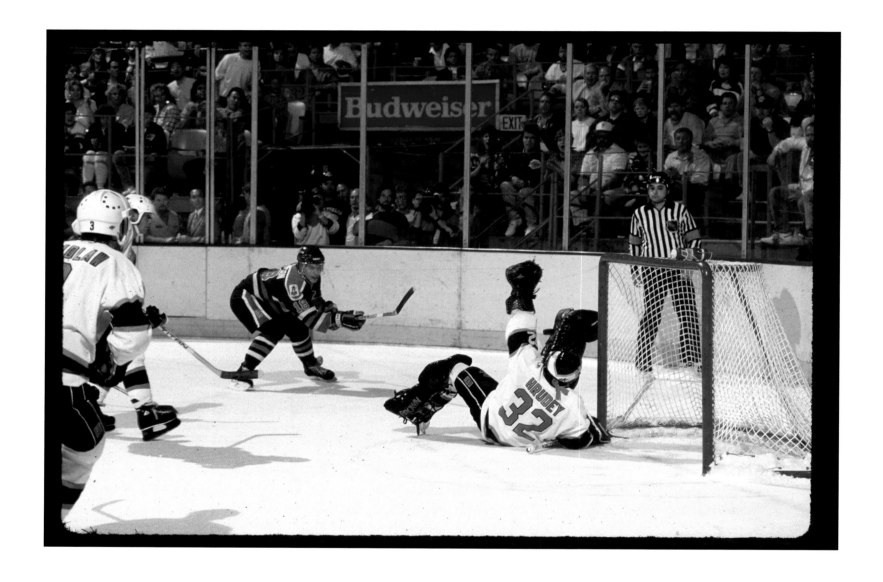

Colourful Kelly Hrudey — sporting his signature blue bandana beneath his mask — makes an unorthodox save against the Oilers' Craig Simpson. Hrudey played 16 NHL seasons, and led the Los Angeles Kings to the 1993 Stanley Cup Final. Like a good many goalies, he went into broadcasting following his career, working alongside the likes of shooter Simpson on hockey telecasts.

Kelly Hrudey

Great Western Forum · Inglewood, CA | 1988-89 ⬦ David E. Klutho | colour · slide · 35mm

In his more than 20 years as a professional hockey player, Lester Patrick played mostly defence, but also spent time at centre, on the wing and even at rover! But he never played goal until Game 2 of the 1928 Stanley Cup Final against the Montreal Maroons, when, as the 44-year-old coach and general manager of the New York Rangers, he was forced to don the pads and enter the fray after goaltender Lorne Chabot sustained an eye injury early in the second period. The Rangers took the game in over-time, 2-1, and the series, with replacement goalie Joe Miller of the New York Americans in net for the remaining games.

Lester Patrick

❧ HHOF 1947 ❧

Madison Square Garden · New York, NY | April 1928 ◯ Hockey Hall of Fame | B/W · print · 7¼" x 9¼"

Remember table-top hockey players? The flash in this photo captures Toronto's
Bill Juzda and Detroit's Ted Lindsay in silhouette fashion, seemingly cutting them
out of the surrounding play. "Terrible Ted," long-time NHL penalty minutes leader,
shown carrying his stick high, was as tough as they come — even though he
came in a 5'8", 160-pound frame!

Ted Lindsay

HHOF 1966

Maple Leafs Gardens · Toronto, ON | March 7, 1951   Imperial Oil - Turofsky | B/W · negative · 4" x 5"

THE ROUGH STUFF

That hockey, especially the professional variety, is a rough and tumble game is a clichéd but still universally accepted truth. It has been since Day One, or at least Day Three.

In its issue of March 3, 1875, previewing what is now considered the first-ever official game of hockey as we know it, the *Montreal Gazette* reported: "A game of hockey will be played at the Victoria Skating Rink this evening by two nines chosen from among the membership. Good fun may be expected as some of the players are reported to be exceedingly expert at the game."

If "good fun" was indeed had during the game, things went downhill rather quickly at some point, at least according to the *Kingston Whig-Standard*, which in its March 5 edition reported: "A disgraceful sight took place at Montreal at the Victoria Skating Rink after a game of hockey. Shins and heads were battered, benches smashed, and the lady spectators fled in confusion."

It is inevitable, really, that passionate and competitive athletes bearing sticks and dashing about on steel blades in what is essentially a caged environment has resulted and continues to result in violent collisions and clashes of all kinds. And that's usually between whistles. That tensions and tempers regularly boil over into less than salubrious and sporting behaviour after the whistle should be no surprise then, either. Hockey players, like everyone else, are flawed, and prone, perhaps more so than other athletes, to "losing their cool," as they say.

The purpose here is not to glorify violence in hockey, but to present captivating photographs that capture the game's inherent intensity and fury and the passions it inflames, as well as the often chaotic, sometimes even comical, scenes it inspires.

Remember these skirmishes?

Brawls were common in the 1970s, and their telltale sign was a sheet
of ice littered with gloves and sticks. This brouhaha occurred between
the Blues and Bruins, a regular occurrence when the two tough teams
got together, and often featured famous St. Louis defenceman Bob
Gassoff (No. 3, far right). The Quesnel, B.C. native amassed 866 penalty
minutes in just 245 NHL games.

Blues vs Bruins

St. Louis Arena · St. Louis, MO | Mid-1970s   Portnoy | colour · slide · 35mm

Some of the Toronto Police Department's finest come
over the boards to help end a bench-clearing brawl in a
game between the Maple Leafs and visiting Chicago Black
Hawks. One of the most famous brawls in NHL history, the
March 11 "Massacre" would eventually end in a 2-2 tie.

Leafs vs Black Hawks

Maple Leaf Gardens · Toronto, ON | March 11, 1961   Imperial Oil - Turofsky | B/W · negative · 4" x 5"

Mixed martial arts may be known for its octagon, but it isn't the first sport to feature caged combatants. That would be hockey, as illustrated in this photo of the fight between New York's Americans and Rangers with the referee in cream-coloured sweater doing his best to regain order.

Americans vs Rangers

Left with no dance partner, Leafs legend and member of the famed "Kid Line," Charlie Conacher, seen here with the New York Americans, looks on as his new teammates tangle with some of his old ones in a 1940 game at Madison Square Garden. A gifted goal scorer, "The Big Bomber" was a key member of the Leafs for nine seasons in the 1930s, and helped them capture the Stanley Cup in 1932. He was inducted into the Hall in 1961.

Leafs vs Americans

They didn't call him "Leapin' Louie" for nothing. New York Rangers defenceman Lou Fontinato gets airborne after his hit on a Toronto player while Andy Hebenton (No. 12) collects the loose puck. Fontinato was one of hockey's biggest hitters and toughest players over nine seasons with the Rangers and Canadiens. In his first full NHL season, 1955-56, his 202 penalty minutes set a new league record.

Lou Fontinato

Maple Leaf Gardens · Toronto, ON | January 16, 1960 ◌ Michael Burns Sr. | B/W · negative · 4" x 5"

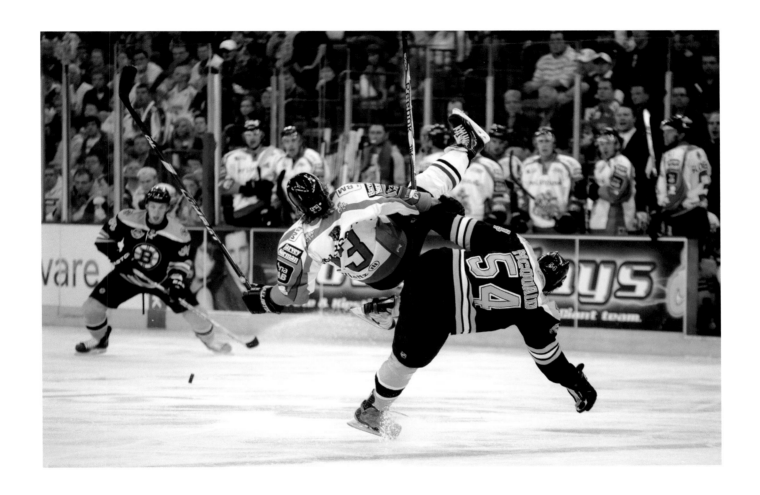

Talk about getting your Irish up. Boston Bruins defenceman
Adam McQuaid sends a member of the Belfast Giants
Elite League Selects flying. The Bruins took on the Selects, a
team of all-stars from the United Kingdom Elite Ice Hockey
League, as part of a pre-season trip to Europe. Boston
prevailed by a score of 5-1. Nine months later, the Bruins
won the Stanley Cup in Vancouver.

Adam McQuaid

Odyssey Arena · Belfast, UK | October 7, 2010   Michael Cooper | colour · digital

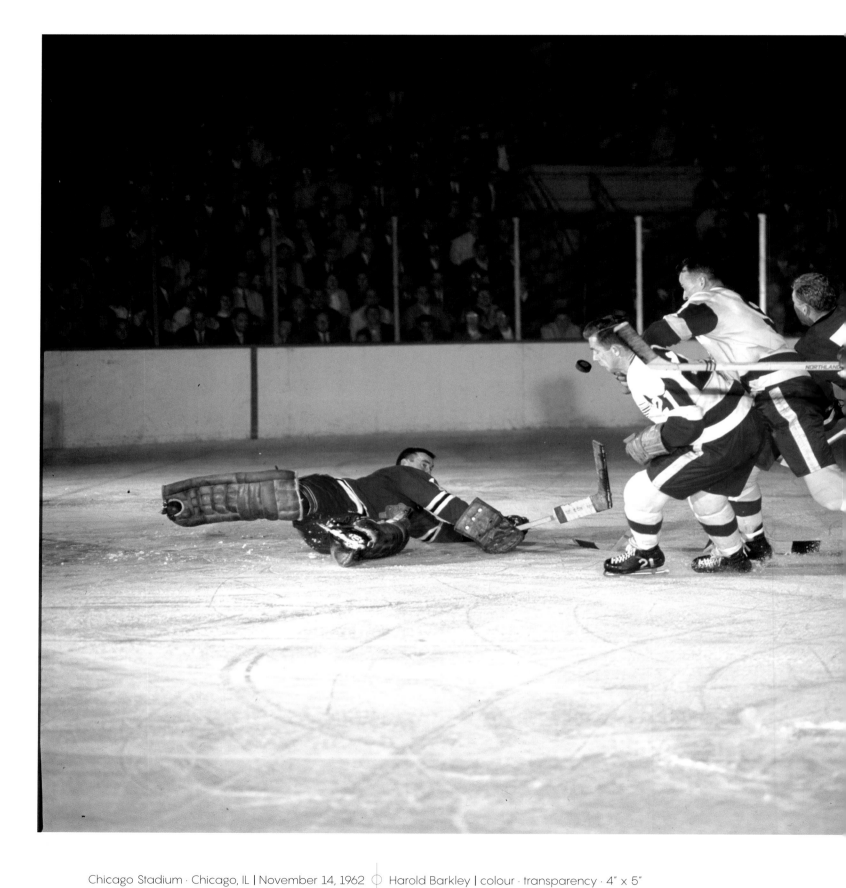

Chicago Stadium · Chicago, IL | November 14, 1962 ⏀ Harold Barkley | colour · transparency · 4" x 5"

One of the latest additions to the Hall of Fame's collection — and to this book — is this personal favourite of famous photographer Harold Barkley, which hasn't been published since it appeared in his own book in 1969. The dynamic action shot shows legend, Gordie Howe being chased down by future legend Bobby Hull (No. 7).

Black Hawks vs Red Wings

S-A-T-U-R-D-A-Y Night! Canadiens forward Phil Goyette has lost his sweater in a donnybrook, only to have teammate Doug Harvey recover it (left). George Hayes tries to separate the combatants in this other game between the Rangers and Canadiens at the Forum (opposite). "Biggest Brawl in Years," read the headline to the game story in the *Montreal Gazette*.

Phil Goyette

Montreal Forum · Montreal, QC | November 30, 1957 ◯ Studio Alain Brouillard | B/W · negative · 4" x 5"

Montreal Forum · Montreal, QC | February 28, 1959 ◇ Studio Alain Brouillard | B/W · negative · 4" x 5"

Maple Leaf Gardens · Toronto, ON | March 19, 1960 ◇ Imperial Oil - Turofsky | B/W · negative · 4" x 5"

Timing is everything in sports — and in sports photography. This photo from the Turofsky collection captures the moment perfectly after Black Hawks defenceman Pierre Pilote (No. 3) flips Leafs forward Gerry James onto his head in front of the Chicago net, guarded by goalie Glenn Hall, as Murray Balfour (No. 8), Elmer "Moose" Vasko (No. 4) and Bobby Hull (No. 16, hidden) look on.

Leafs vs Black Hawks

Linesman George Hayes was colourful, controversial and a trendsetter. He began officiating in 1946 and was the first NHL official to amass 1,000 games. The big, smooth-skating Hayes was known for his humour, flouting league rules (he was once fined for not shaving) and for scrapbooking. He was the first linesman to hand the puck over to his fellow officials at face-offs, instead of tossing it or sliding it along the ice. Hayes' NHL career ended in 1965 after being suspended indefinitely by league president Clarence Campbell for refusing to take an eye test mandated for league officials.

George Hayes

HHOF 1988

Maple Leaf Gardens · Toronto, ON | c.1951-52   Imperial Oil-Turofsky | B/W · negative · 4" x 5"

There's a Ford in your future, Taylor Hall. Florida's Jonathan Marchessault
takes out the New Jersey Devil in this photo from the 2016-17 season.
Hall, a native of Calgary whose family later moved to Kingston, Ontario,
was selected first overall by the Edmonton Oilers in the 2010 NHL
Entry Draft. He was traded to New Jersey in the summer of 2016 for
defenceman Adam Larsson.

Taylor Hall

The old adage was true even back in the old days. If you're going to go to the net in the NHL, you have to be willing to pay the price. Here, a total of seven Leafs and Rangers — and one referee — vie for positioning during a goalmouth scramble with goalie "Gump" Worsley coolly in control of things.

Leafs vs Rangers

Maple Leaf Gardens · Toronto, ON | December 13, 1958 ○ Imperial Oil-Turofsky | B/W · negative · 4" x 5"

CLASSIC PHOTOS

Alternately known as "The Entertainer" or "The Nose," Eddie Shack
was a showman, spokesman and journeyman playing for six NHL
teams, including, most famously, the Leafs. He also had a hit song
written about him, "Clear the Track, Here Comes Shack," a tune
California Seals' Gerry Ehman clearly hadn't heard before taking
the popular Shack for a ride…on his back.

Eddie Shack & Gerry Ehman

Buffalo Memorial Auditorium · Buffalo, NY | 1970-71   Bob Shaver | B/W · negative · 35mm

Perhaps more than most professional athletes,
hockey players are happy to engage their fans
with no better illustration than this charming shot
of Flames favourite Joe Nieuwendyk signing
autographs from atop the Calgary players'
bench in the Olympic Saddledome.

Joe Nieuwendyk

HHOF 2011

Olympic Saddledome · Calgary, AB | Undated ○ David E. Klutho | colour · slide · 35mm

FANS & RINKS

From the equipment its players wear to the rules it is played under, and the expansion of the NHL from four teams in Canada to a 31-team league that reaches into just about every corner of North America, so much about hockey has changed in the past century. The one constant over the past 100 years has been the support the game receives from its fans. Without its supporters, there would be no hockey, at least not NHL hockey, anyway.

Since December 19, 1917, when supporters in Montreal celebrated the NHL's first-ever goal, by Dave Ritchie of the Montreal Wanderers, fans have travelled by foot, car, subway train, trolley and tram and reached into their pockets for money, money that was at times scarce, to buy tickets for the games their heroes played. They have clapped, cheered and stomped their feet, hooted, hollered and booed as they let the game lift them up, or let them down…and sometimes carry them away.

As a number of these photos show, there was a time before the era of multi-million-dollar contracts when contact between the fans and the players was not so closely managed, and the line between participant and observer was not so wide. Sometimes, when the glass and wire that separated the stands from the ice were not so high, or didn't exist at all, as some of these photos also reveal, the fans even become part of the action.

The famous rinks, like the beloved Montreal Forum, Maple Leaf Gardens, Chicago Stadium and Boston Garden, have changed, too. In fact, just about all of the original "barns" are gone (certainly the Original Six arenas) but not forgotten by those who watched hockey games inside them. Photos of these buildings, and more importantly, the happy, sad and sometimes angry fans that filled the seats, are like time capsules.

Remembering simpler times!

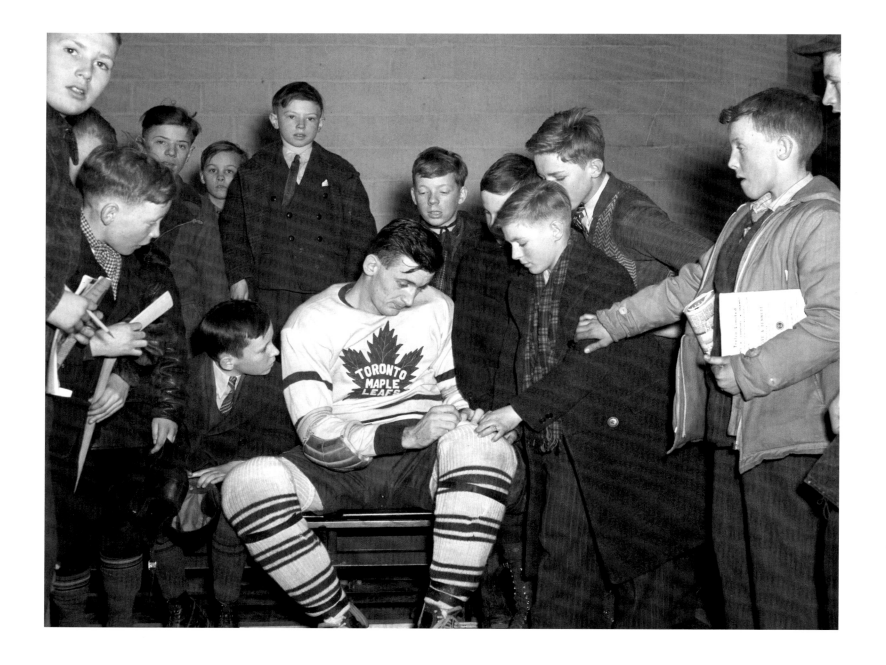

Have you ever seen such polite autograph hounds? This group of young, well-dressed fans gather around for a signing session with Toronto forward John McCormack at Maple Leaf Gardens, with half paying close attention to the actual signature and the other half more focused on the photographer. McCormack, nicknamed "Goose" for his long neck, played 84 games with the Leafs between 1948 and 1951.

John McCormack

Maple Leaf Gardens · Toronto, ON | Early 1950s ⬦ Imperial Oil-Turofsky | B/W · negative · 4" x 5"

A young Frank Mahovlich of the Toronto Maple Leafs, the evening's First Star, and Andy Hebenton of the New York Rangers sign autographs for fans as they wait for their names to be called following a late 1950s game at Maple Leaf Gardens. "The Big M" was the NHL's Rookie-of-the-Year in 1958 and went on to score 40-plus goals with three different NHL teams. Mahovlich was named a Canadian Senator in 1998.

Frank Mahovlich

HHOF 1981

Players' safety when it comes to hostile fans on the road wasn't necessarily a big issue back in the days, as illustrated in this photo of visiting Detroit Red Wings on the players bench at the Montreal Forum.

Detroit Red Wings

Montreal Forum · Montreal, QC | March 5, 1960 ○ Studio Alain Brouillard | B/W · negative · 4" x 5"

Marcel Pronovost (No. 3) of the Detroit Red Wings appears to have words with a fan during a game. Maple Leaf Gardens became the first NHL rink to replace the chicken wire behind the nets and in the corners with Plexiglas, but the space above the boards remained open for a number of years, allowing for up-close-and-personal fan-player interactions. Glass eventually found its way atop the boards in every NHL rink, but it was low enough for fans to be able to reach up and grab players' sticks. Higher glass was installed in the early 1980s.

Marcel Pronovost

HHOF 1978

Montreal Forum · Montreal, QC | January 4, 1958   Studio Alain Brouillard | B/W · negative · 4" x 5"

Chicago Stadium · Chicago, IL | April 6, 1961 ⓒ Le Studio du Hockey | B/W · negative · 2¼" x 2¼"

Fans line up around the block to enter Chicago Stadium, the raucously loud "Madhouse on Madison" and home of the Chicago Black Hawks from its opening in 1929 until its closing in 1994. Built at a cost of $9.5 million, the Stadium was the largest indoor arena in the world at the time of its construction, with a capacity of 16,000 for hockey and 17,000 for basketball. The building featured a 3,663-pipe Barton organ with the world's largest console (six keyboards). It was also the last NHL venue to have an analog game clock (a Bulova, from 1943 to 1975).

Chicago Stadium

While the hometown Bruins might
have considered the Boston Garden
small and intimate, you can rest as-
sured visiting teams saw the famous
North End arena differently.

Boston Garden

Boston Garden · Boston, MA | Late 1960s ○ Frank Prazak | colour · slide · 35mm

East Division goaltender Tony Esposito (the 'A' on the back of his jersey is for Anthony) leaves his net to beat onrushing West Division forward Bill Goldsworthy to the puck during the 1970 NHL All-Star Game, while Brad Park (No. 3) comes back to help. The game was the first All-Star Game to be broadcast live on U.S. network television. The East Division won 4-1. Esposito's teammate on the Chicago Black Hawks, Bobby Hull, was MVP.

Tony Esposito

HHOF 1988

New York Islanders captain Bryan Trottier salutes
the team's fans in this magical moment during
the dying seconds of Game 4 of the 1983 Stanley
Cup Final. The Islanders defeated the Oilers by a
score of 4-2 to sweep the best-of-seven series
and win their fourth consecutive Stanley Cup.
Trottier scored the game's first goal.

Bryan Trottier

HHOF 1997

Nassau Veterans Memorial Coliseum · Uniondale, NY | May 17, 1983 ⏐ Paul Bereswill | colour · slide · 35mm

CLASSIC PHOTOS

Guy "The Flower" Lafleur was famous for bringing the Montreal Forum faithful out of their seats with his daring rushes. His flying blond mane, once he removed his helmet at the start of the 1974-75 season, would become a bonus for Habs fans, eliciting chants of "Guy, Guy, Guy!"

Guy Lafleur

❧ HHOF 1988 ❧

Montreal Forum · Montreal, QC | 1973-74 ⟡ Frank Prazak | colour · transparency · 2¼" x 2¼"

Longtime Toronto Maple Leafs trainer Tim Daly (standing) and his assistant, Tommy Nayler, use a sewing machine to sew a "C" onto the sweater of Leafs captain Ted Kennedy. Daly's service to the team pre-dates the Maple Leafs' name. He started his career as the trainer for the Toronto St. Pats in 1926 and kept the position until he retired in 1960. Nayler had a knack for customizing equipment, and a reputation for being the best skate sharpener in the business.

Tim Daly & Tommy Nayler

Maple Leaf Gardens · Toronto, ON | 1948-49   Imperial Oil-Turofsky | B/W · negative · 4" x 5"

BEHIND *the* SCENES

Most of the action in hockey takes place out on the ice, but a lot goes on behind the scenes, much of it banal, some of it humorous and some of it as exciting as the games themselves. Fortunately, cameras have been providing fascinating glimpses into what goes on in the hallways, dressing rooms and assorted nooks and crannies of NHL rinks since the game's early days. In fact, back when it was more of a game and the stakes were not quite so high, those who chronicled it in photographs faced fewer restrictions and therefore had more access. These are the results of that access.

The hockey dressing room is a place to prepare, or unwind. Many of the dressing room photos that follow also offer a glimpse at what players wore in battle, like Leafs legend "Turk" Broda's leather pads. Then there's fellow netminder Glenn Hall's flimsy chest protector, which he wore while facing down powerful players like Gordie Howe and Bernie "Boom-Boom" Geoffrion. No wonder he smoked. Consider too Maurice "Rocket" Richard and his heavy stick with its straight blade, the better to whip a hard backhand at the likes of Broda and Hall.

These photos also reveal why we call them "dressing rooms" and not "locker rooms" as they are called in other sports. Look beyond the players depicted in them and you'll find plaques on the wall, clothing on hooks, racks of sticks, chairs, benches, stalls and fedoras, plenty of fedoras…but no lockers (with one exception).

Some of the photos here are obviously staged, others, thanks to the more relaxed atmosphere of the time, capture truly unguarded moments. Both have their charms.

Join us behind the scenes.

Walter "Turk" Broda poses with his goaltending equipment. Like most of his netminding colleagues, the Maple Leafs legend used pads made by Emil "Pops" Kenesky in his sporting goods store in Hamilton, Ontario. Kenesky made his first pair of pads in 1924 for Hamilton Tigers goalie Jackie Forbes. The bigger more protective pads soon caught on, and Keneskys were soon the pads of choice for professional hockey goalies. Based on the design of cricket pads, Kenesky's were made of horsehide and generously filled with deer hair and later furniture stuffing.

Turk Broda

HHOF 1967

Maple Leaf Gardens · Toronto, ON | Undated ⌀ Imperial Oil - Turofsky | B/W · negative · 4" x 5"

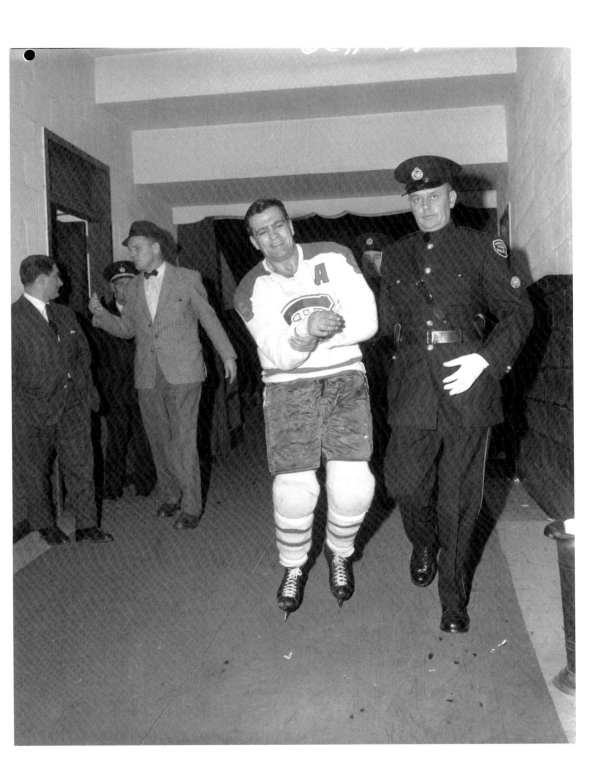

Bernie "Boom-Boom" Geoffrion is helped to the dressing room by security after injuring his wrist. The oft-injured "Boomer" is said to have broken his nose nine times during his 16-year career, and received hundreds of stitches as well. A six-time Stanley Cup champion, and owner of one of hockey's hardest shots (thus the nickname), he enjoyed his best season in 1960-61, becoming only the second player in history to score 50 goals in a season and winning both the Art Ross and Hart trophies as top scorer and MVP.

Bernie Geoffrion

HHOF 1972

Maurice "Rocket" Richard of the Montreal Canadiens inspects the straight blade of his hockey stick. Richard used Hespeler and Northland Pro sticks at various times early in his career and later played with a CCM Pattern Made Professional model supplied by a local sporting goods store. Wooden sticks from this era, typically made of ash, like baseball bats, weighed approximately 25 ounces.

Maurice Richard

HHOF 1961

Maple Leaf Gardens · Toronto, ON | Undated ○ Imperial Oil - Turofsky | B/W · negative · 4" x 5"

Bobby Rousseau of the Montreal
Canadiens tapes his stick prior to a
game. The Habs dressing room was
famous for honouring past greats from
whom current players were passed
the torch "to hold it high."

Bobby Rousseau

Montreal Forum · Montreal, QC | Early 1960s   Studio Alain Brouillard | B/W · negative · 2¼" x 2¼"

Maple Leaf Gardens · Toronto, ON | February 2, 1935 ⦶ Imperial Oil – Turofsky | B/W · glass · 4" x 5"

New York Americans goaltender Roy Worters, (right, enjoying a cigarette) and Toronto netminder George Hainsworth after a 1935 game at Maple Leaf Gardens. Five years earlier, the Americans loaned Worters to the Montreal Canadiens for one game to replace the ailing Hainsworth. The Hart Trophy winner of 1929 (a first for a goalie) and the Vezina Trophy winner of 1931, Worters helped Montreal win the game in question, a 6-2 win over Toronto on February 27, 1930, while Hainsworth was laid up in hospital recovering from the flu. At 5'3", Worters, nicknamed "Shrimp," is the shortest ever NHL player.

George Hainsworth & Roy Worters

HHOF 1961   **HHOF 1969**

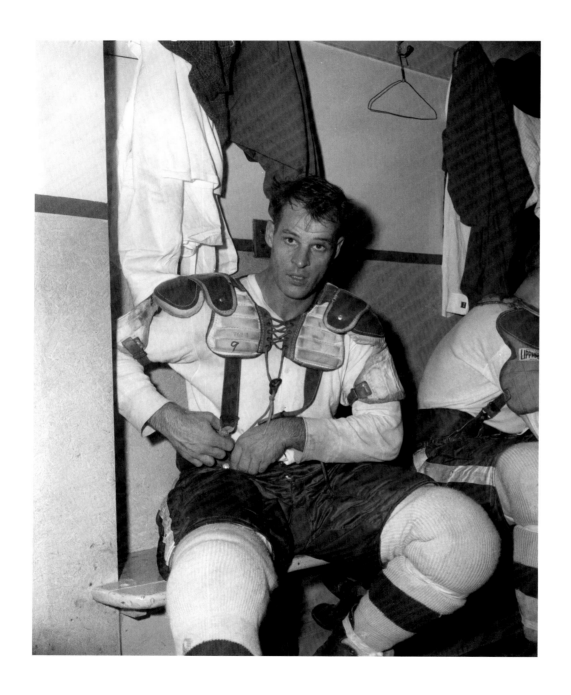

The first shoulder and elbow pads used by NHLers were made of felt and leather. Those gave way to more protective models with hard plastic shells. However, after a spate of facial injuries primarily caused by flying elbows, which Gordie Howe may have had something to do with, the NHL ordered that all pads must have a soft outer covering. "Mr. Hockey" was an offensive power (1,850 points in 1,767 NHL games) who amassed 1,685 career penalty minutes.

Gordie Howe

HHOF 1972

Montreal Forum · Montreal, QC | November 20, 1958   Studio Alain Brouillard | B/W · negative · 4″ x 5″

Aubrey Victor "Dit" Clapper of the Boston Bruins pulls on his sweater before a game. Between 1936 and 1948, the Bruins sweater featured player numbers on both the front and back. Clapper played 20 seasons in Boston, starring as both forward and defenceman between 1927 and 1947, and served as player-coach for one season and head coach for three more. At 6'2" and 200 lbs, he was one of the biggest NHL players of his time. The only player to win three Stanley Cup championships as a Bruin, Clapper's nickname stems from his inability to pronounce his own name, Vic, as a young child.

Dit Clapper

HHOF 1947

Toronto Maple Leafs rookie Dick Duff, head coach King Clancy and general manager Hap Day celebrate the 19-year-old's first NHL goal. Duff, who would go on to win the Stanley Cup six times (two with Toronto and four with Montreal) in a career that spanned more than 20 seasons, wore No. 17 when he first arrived in Toronto, but was given the No. 9 shortly after the retirement of Leafs captain Ted "Teeder" Kennedy.

Dick Duff

HHOF 2006

Maple Leaf Gardens · Toronto, ON | October 26, 1955 ⬦ Imperial Oil-Turofsky | B/W · negative · 4" x 5"

Prior to the 1980-81 season, only one player had scored
50 goals in 50 games — a certain Maurice Richard. Fellow
Quebecer Mike Bossy would match the legendary Rocket's
feat in the Islanders' 50th game, scoring two goals to add
to his 48, including No. 50 with 1:29 remaining against the
Quebec Nordiques' Ron Grahame.

Mike Bossy

HHOF 1991

Glenn Hall of the Chicago Black Hawks smokes a post-game cigarette. It may come as a surprise in this day and age of proper exercise and nutrition, but smoking was common among hockey players well into the 1980s, as was the drinking of soda pop in the pre-sports-drink era. Like other goalies before him, the notoriously anxious Hall may have "sparked one up" after games to help calm his shaky nerves.

Glenn Hall

HHOF 1975

Montreal Forum · Montreal, QC | October 10, 1957   Studio Alain Brouillard | B/W · negative · 4" x 5"

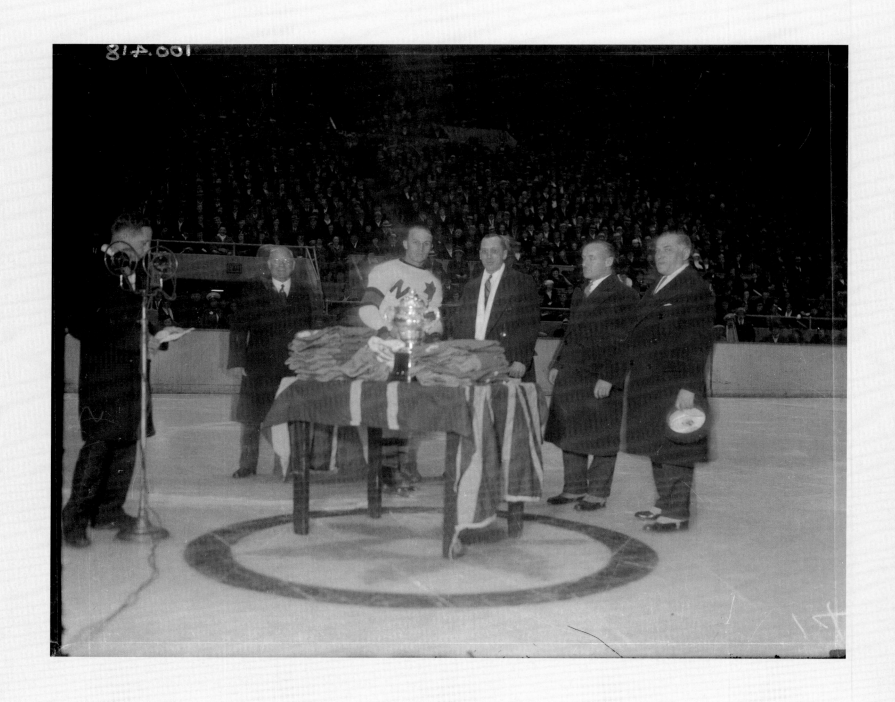

Maple Leaf Gardens · Toronto, ON | February 14, 1934 ◯ Imperial Oil – Turofsky | B/W · glass · 4" x 5"

BOSTON - MAR. 6 1934

BOSTON VS. LEAFS
1 2

The NHL's first All-Star Game was perhaps its most emotional. Known as the Ace Bailey Benefit Game, it was played to raise money for Bailey whose career was ended by a hit from Eddie Shore during the 1933-34 season. The game was won by the Maple Leafs against a team of NHL All-Stars (opposite). Bailey had recovered from his head injury to attend the game. The photo at left shows the dramatic moment later that season when the Leafs' Bailey and the Bruins' Shore shook hands in Boston.

Ace Bailey & Eddie Shore

❧ HHOF 1975 ❧   ❧ HHOF 1947 ❧

Boston Garden · Boston, MA | March 6, 1934 ⬡ Le Studio du Hockey | B/W · print · 8" x 10"

William Scott "Scotty" Bowman, the most successful coach in NHL history, poses with the five replica Stanley Cups he won with the Montreal Canadiens. The demanding bench boss left the Canadiens after their fourth consecutive Cup in 1979 to take over as coach and general manager of the Buffalo Sabres, where he remained until 1987. He would replace the ailing Bob Johnson as head coach of the defending champion Pittsburgh Penguins in 1991, when he went on to win his sixth Cup. He captured three more championships with the Detroit Red Wings. Bowman's ninth and final Stanley Cup in 2002 saw him break the record long held by his mentor, "Toe" Blake.

Scotty Bowman

HHOF 1991

Bowman home · Buffalo, NY | February 3, 1984   Paul Bereswill | colour · slide · 35mm

COLOURFUL COACHES

In hockey, the players usually get the glory, and the coaches often get the grief. That's just the way it is, in bad times more than good ones, anyhow. But in the course of hockey history, many coaches have emerged to become household names in their own right, some by their success and longevity, others by their colourful personalities.

Many of them ex-players themselves, hockey coaches are often fascinating characters that pull the strings from behind the bench — usually in their own style. Some are natural-born leaders and motivational experts, others brilliant tacticians. The best tend to combine both.

The photos that follow show some of the game's bench bosses at work. Many, like former police officer Pat Burns, were stern figures. The most successful among them, like nine-time Stanley Cup winner Scotty Bowman, could be impatient and aloof. Others, like Philadelphia Flyers legend Freddie "The Fog" Shero and Roger Neilson, were as quirky and colourful as the sweatsuits they wore while running practices. Some were detested by their players, while others were loved. All of the above shared a passion for the game.

Bowman and his mentor, Hector "Toe" Blake, had long successful runs behind the bench, while American legends Herb Brooks and "Badger" Bob Johnson, who famously declared every day a "great day for hockey," left us too soon but left lasting legacies nonetheless. Perhaps the most famous hockey coach of all, Don Cherry, who has been telling it like it is from his famous 'Coach's Corner' on 'Hockey Night in Canada' for parts of four decades, only coached in the NHL for six seasons. But he'll always be "Coach" to his generations of followers.

So here they are, under their fedoras or ball caps, in leather, satin or nylon team jackets, in suits of pinstripes and plaid, both single- and double-breasted.

Remembering the game's Colourful Coaches.

"Win today and we walk together forever," Fred Shero once said. And he knew a thing or two about winning. The enigmatic coach of the Philadelphia Flyers and New York Rangers for 10 seasons in the 1970s won titles in the International, Central and American hockey leagues before making the jump to the NHL in 1971 and winning back-to-back Cups with the Flyers in 1974 and 1975. Nicknamed "Freddie the Fog" for often seeming to be lost in thought, Shero was actually a brilliant strategist and innovator unafraid to try something new, like having players practise in tracksuits.

Fred Shero
HHOF 2013

The Spectrum · Philadelphia, PA | November 1974 ○ Frank Prazak | colour · slide · 35mm

The New York Rangers' first coach, Lester Patrick stepped away from the bench in 1939 to concentrate on his duties as general manager and team president. His replacement was Frank Boucher, the legendary Rangers star of the 1920s and '30s who had been apprenticing with the Rangers' Eastern Hockey League farm team, the New York Rovers. In his first year behind the Rangers bench, he led the team to its third Stanley Cup. Boucher coached the team for 10 years. In 1946, he succeeded Patrick as GM, a position he held until 1955.

Frank Boucher

HHOF 1958

Location Unknown | 1940s ◊ Le Studio du Hockey | B/W · print · 8" x 10"

Hector "Toe" Blake trades his trademark suit and fedora for a cap and team jacket. Blake won 11 Stanley Cup championships during his NHL career, 10 of them with the Montreal Canadiens. He won three Cups as a player, the first as a member of the Montreal Maroons in 1935, and then two more, with the Habs. He then won eight more over 13 seasons as the Canadiens' coach. Stern and demanding, he was also a brilliant student of the game. Blake hated to lose as reflected by his record: his teams lost only 292 of the combined 1,033 regular season and playoff games he coached.

Toe Blake

HHOF 1966

Location Unknown | Late 1960s   O-Pee-Chee | colour · transparency · 2¼" x 2¾"

Of all the colourful coaches in NHL history, and there have been a few, none have matched the bombast and notoriety of Don Cherry. Two-time Stanley Cup finalist with his beloved Bruins, and 1976 Coach of the Year, "Grapes" has enjoyed an even more successful career playing a coach on TV with his 'Coach's Corner' segment garnering much-watch status on hockey broadcasts.

Don Cherry

Pacific Coliseum · Vancouver, BC | November 11, 1983 Paul Bereswill | colour · slide · 35mm

The colourful and quirky leader of eight NHL teams, Roger Neilson, was one of the most unusual and beloved coaches in history. Nicknamed "Captain Video" for his pioneering use of game film, he led Vancouver to the 1982 Stanley Cup Final. After three winning seasons with the New York Rangers, Neilson was fired partway through the fourth, in 1993, then looked on from Florida as the Rangers won the Stanley Cup in 1994. Following two years in Philadelphia, where he was diagnosed with bone cancer in 1999, he signed on as an assistant with Ottawa for the 2001-02 season. Senators coach Jacques Martin stepped aside for the season's final two games, allowing Neilson to take over and reach the 1,000-game milestone. He succumbed to cancer at age 69 in June 2003.

Roger Neilson

HHOF 2002

When Scotty Bowman replaced Bob Johnson behind the bench in Pittsburgh in 1991, the Penguins players found out the true meaning of culture shock. For if Bowman was one of the most difficult coaches in hockey, Johnson was probably its nicest. Nicknamed "Badger Bob" for his long tenure at the University of Wisconsin, and a firm believer that every day was a "great day for hockey," Johnson served as the president of USA Hockey from 1987 to 1990. He would lead Pittsburgh to the first Stanley Cup in its history in the 1990-91 season. Johnson was stricken by brain cancer a few months later and died in November 1991.

Bob Johnson

HHOF 1992

Player, coach, general manager, president: Glen "Slats" Sather has done it all at the NHL level, including winning four Stanley Cup championships with the Edmonton Oilers, in the 1980s, as head coach, and five overall. He was also coach of the Oilers in the WHA prior to the team joining the NHL in 1979.

Glen Sather

HHOF 1997

He is remembered mostly for the role he played in the greatest upset in hockey history, but Herb Brooks spent several seasons in the NHL after that miracle moment in 1980. After coaching in Switzerland, Brooks coached the New York Rangers for parts of four seasons. He then returned to Minnesota, where he led the University of Minnesota Golden Gophers to three NCAA national championships between 1972-79. He led the Minnesota North Stars for a single season, 1987-88, before coaching parts of two more NHL seasons, in New Jersey and for the last 58 games of the 1999-2000 season in Pittsburgh. Brooks died in an auto accident at age 66, in 2003.

Herb Brooks

HHOF 2006

Met Center · Bloomington, MN | 1987-88 ♀ David E. Klutho | colour · slide · 35mm

With his roots in working-class Montreal and extensive background in police work, Pat Burns was never going to be anything but a tough, team-first disciplinarian as an NHL coach. Burns was also a winner, taking the Canadiens to the Stanley Cup Final and winning the Jack Adams Award as Coach of the Year, in 1988, a feat he replicated in Toronto in 1993 and in Boston in 1998. In 2002-03, he led the Devils to the Stanley Cup. Burns passed away from cancer at the age of 58 in 2010.

Pat Burns

HHOF 2014

Renowned hockey photographer and innovator Harold Barkley goes over the details of a photo shoot with Jean Béliveau of the Montreal Canadiens. Barkley, who joined the staff of the *Toronto Star* in 1958, pioneered colour action hockey photography with his use of spotlighting via powerful strobe lights synchronized to his cameras. He lugged his equipment, which weighed about 350 pounds, to all six of the Original Six cities, but could most often be found working at Maple Leaf Gardens. Barkley's best-known work appeared in the *Star Weekly*, a popular colour supplement to the newspaper, and his photos later found their way into the pages of *Hockey Illustrated*, *Time*, and *Sports Illustrated*.

Maple Leaf Gardens · Toronto, ON | Undated ◯ Harold Barkley | B/W · digital copy · 2¼" x 2¼"

SHOOTING THE GAME

Before every NHL game was televised and cameras equipped with zoom lenses as long as your arm could bring a bead of sweat into sharp focus from 100 feet away, the photographers who chronicled hockey had to make do with the equipment they had, as bulky and heavy as it was. They more than got by over the years thanks to their own ingenuity and an access to the action on the ice that would be unheard of today. In many cases, the images they captured possess a stark beauty worthy of a museum or art gallery wall.

The game's first cameramen were more like old-time newspaper photographers than sports specialists, often strolling out onto the ice, huge cameras in hand, to shoot fight and injury scenes like they were car crashes. Those who wanted to capture the actual game action set up as close to the ice as possible, in open spots along the boards and in corners, shooting through holes cut in the protective wire or glass.

Early photos were often dark, with only weak arena lighting and camera flash bulbs illuminating the scene. Flashes were soon mounted high on the glass, and later, strobe lights installed above the ice surface provided better lighting as black and white gave way to colour. Soon, cameras fired by remote controls would be installed above and even inside the nets.

Promotional photography was another thing altogether. In the beginning, it was crude, with uniformed players hauled outdoors to be photographed against brick walls or other basic backgrounds. To simulate action, complex scenes were staged out on the ice, where players were asked to strike and hold poses replicating ferocious body checks and other collisions.

Today's games are chronicled by professionals working with state-of-the-art equipment. At special events, like the annual outdoor games, video cameras travel along cables to follow the action up ice. Photographers can now fire off thousands of shots per game and then quickly scroll through them to select the best ones. Their pioneering counterparts, on the other hand, could afford no such luxury, and had to rely on their knowledge of the game and the players to get the perfect shot. Both methods could produce stunning results. Shooting the game was, and still is, an art form.

Such great memories.

This newspaper photographer wants to get close, but not too close, to the fight taking place between members of the Toronto Maple Leafs and Boston Bruins. Boston captain Milt Schmidt (No. 15) appears to be one of the combatants.

Maple Leaf Gardens · Toronto, ON | March 31, 1951   Imperial Oil - Turofsky | B/W · negative · 4" x 5"

Before the members of the Stanley Cup-winning Montreal Canadiens can even hit the ice in celebration, a newspaper photographer has beaten them to it. In a time before powerful zoom lenses and other technological advances, hockey photographers had to be as physically close as possible to the action they wanted to capture on film. This game, giving the Habs their record fifth Cup in a row, was the last for Maurice Richard, wearing the "C," on the bench next to coach Toe Blake. Toronto's Tim Horton (No. 7), looks on.

Maple Leaf Gardens · Toronto, ON | April 14, 1960 ◇ Michael Burns Sr. | B/W · negative · 4" x 5"

Maple Leaf Gardens · Toronto, ON | March 20, 1948 ⏀ Imperial Oil - Turofsky | B/W · negative · 4" x 5"

To capture the game from a different perspective, photographers might perch in the stands behind the nets when possible. In this photo, the camera flash is illuminating the logo in the middle of the puck, tracked by goalie Harry Lumley; Ted Lindsay and Gordie Howe of the Red Wings and Vic Lynn of the Maple Leafs are part of the action. Lumley was inducted into the Hall in 1980.

Dave Kryskow of the Atlanta Flames (No. 8) and
Bob MacMillan of the St. Louis Blues (No. 21) prepare to jump into play in this unique faceoff shot
taken at ice level at the St. Louis Arena during the
1975-76 season. The Blues would prevail, 7-3.

St. Louis Arena · St. Louis, MO | October 25, 1975 ○ Portnoy | colour · slide · 35mm

John Zimmerman of *Sports Illustrated* became the first photographer to place a camera inside a net to shoot an NHL hockey game, capturing the action between the New York Rangers and Montreal Canadiens. He triggered his camera remotely from a wire running under the ice. In 1966, Barton Silverman, used a similar approach, having a special wooden box built to protect the camera he used. Not to be outdone, Frank Prazak of *Weekend Magazine* built his own five-inch camera for the assignment, and padded it to protect any players who might crash into the net.

Pacific Coliseum · Vancouver, BC | November 30, 1971 ◯ Frank Prazak | colour · slide · 35mm

This staged photo shot during Detroit's training
camp was meant to depict the rough and tumble
nature of NHL hockey. Members of the Red Wings
were all too happy to play their part.

Location Unknown | Undated Frank Prazak | B/W · negative · 35mm

A group of hockey photographers and cinema photographers capture the presentation of the Stanley Cup following Game 4 of the 1960 Final between Montreal and Toronto. The Canadiens won the game 4-0, sweeping the series.

Maple Leaf Gardens · Toronto, ON | April 14, 1960 ○ Imperial Oil-Turofsky | B/W · negative · 2¼" x 2¼"

The Bruins' Marty Barry, the Leafs' Hap Day, Lieutenant
Governor of Ontario Herbert Bruce, Maple Leaf Gardens
President J. P. Bickell and NHL President Frank Calder are
shown prior to a game between Boston and Toronto. Barry
and Day were inducted into the Hockey Hall of Fame in
1965 and 1961, respectively.

Maple Leaf Gardens · Toronto, ON | November 9, 1933 ⏀ Imperial Oil - Turofsky | B/W · glass · 4" x 5"

The famed Turofsky brothers are shown on the other side of their own lens — it's a self-portrait — with their even more famous subject. Lou (left) and Nat Turofsky were preeminent photographers of their day, working tirelessly on all fronts in the Toronto area, particularly the sports scene. Athletes themselves, they were said to possess the instincts necessary to capture sports action, anticipating plays as they developed. Their hockey collection — some 19,000 images — is said to be the largest in the world and is entrusted to the Hockey Hall of Fame.

Maple Leaf Gardens · Toronto, ON | 1951 ♀ Imperial Oil - Turofsky | B/W · negative · 4" x 5"

London, Ontario-based O-Pee-Chee chewing gum company, working in conjunction with the Topps company in the U.S., produced annual sets of NHL player trading cards. Hired photographers would make the rounds of NHL training camps and photograph each player and send the results to the production office. The original photos were often taken outdoors for better light quality and retouched later. This photo of Bill Gadsby of the New York Rangers appeared in the Topps set for the 1959-60 season, minus the countryside in the background. He was inducted into the Hall in 1970.

Location Unknown | Late 1950s ⊘ O-Pee-Chee | colour · transparency · 2¼" x 2¼"

Get this man some skate guards! Dick
Irvin, first star and top scorer of the
Chicago Black Hawks in the team's
inaugural season (1926-27), poses for
a promotional photo of sorts. Although
this photo's exact origins are unknown,
this image of Irvin did appear on an
"All-Time Greats" card in a 1960 Topps
set, but in illustrated form, with a more
suitable backdrop. He was inducted
into the Hockey Hall of Fame in 1958.

Hibbing, MN | 1926-27   Le Studio du Hockey | B/W · print · 8" x 10"

Hockey photographers like Bruce Bennett took the inside the net technique to new levels with the advent of wireless remotes to fire cameras. Today, digital cameras are installed inside protective boxes mounted at the base of the centre bar in the back of the net. Dave Sandford, another netcam pioneer who built the first protective camera boxes approved by the NHL, took this photo of Pittsburgh's Dan Kesa trying to score against Buffalo's Dominik Hasek. Hasek was inducted into the Hockey Hall of Fame in 2014.

Marine Midland Arena · Buffalo, NY | March 28, 1999 ○ Dave Sandford | colour · slide · 35mm

Until the mid-1960s, most hockey action photos were taken from the corners of the rink so photographers could be close to the action swirling around the net. Camera flashes mounted on or above the glass helped illuminate the scene, and openings for the camera lenses were cut in the protective glass or chicken wire. Note the photographer and the flashes in the corner opposite the photographer responsible for this photo in a game between the Maple Leafs and Bruins. The Boston goaltender is "Sugar" Jim Henry. Toronto's No. 4 is Harry Watson, who was inducted into the Hockey Hall of Fame in 1994.

Maple Leaf Gardens · Toronto, ON | 1951-52   Imperial Oil-Turofsky | B/W · negative · 4" x 5"

A photographer has selected and cropped this photo for publication in a newspaper or magazine, and with good reason. He's caught this hip check thrown by Toronto Maple Leafs defenceman Bill Barilko on Milt Schmidt (inducted in 1961) of the Boston Bruins perfectly. Barilko's defence partner is Wally Stanowski.

Maple Leaf Gardens · Toronto, ON | February 8, 1947   Imperial Oil – Turofsky | B/W · negative · 4" x 5"

Boston Garden · Boston, MA | May 24, 1988 ◯ Paul Bereswill | colour · slide · 35mm

CLASSIC PHOTOS

The night the lights went out in Boston. On May 24, 1988, leading the Stanley Cup Final 3-0, the Edmonton Oilers were looking for a sweep of the Boston Bruins and their second consecutive championship. The Bruins and Oilers were tied 3-3 late in the second period when a power failure plunged the Boston Garden into darkness. For security reasons, the Garden was evacuated (left) and the game eventually cancelled. With an NBA game scheduled for the arena the following night, the series moved to Edmonton two nights later for what would have been Game 5. The Oilers won the game, 6-3, and the series, 4-0.

Oilers vs Bruins

Northlands Coliseum · Edmonton, AB | May 26, 1988 ⏀ Paul Bereswill | colour · slide · 35mm

A classic shot of Toronto Maple Leafs coach George "Punch" Imlach savouring his glass of champagne and the prospect of a day off shortly after the Leafs beat the Montreal Canadiens to win the 1963 Stanley Cup. Imlach earned his curious nickname during his junior playing career. After an elbow knocked him cold, he's said to have jumped to his feet, taking a swing at the team trainer who'd come out onto the ice to help him.

Punch Imlach

HHOF 1984

Maple Leaf Gardens · Toronto, ON | April 18, 1963   Graphic Artists | B/W · negative · 4" x 5"

Winning!

Winning. It's the reason the game is played in the first place. For professionals, it's everything.

Despite the underlying stress inherent in high-stakes hockey — or maybe because of it — the emotional release associated with winning can produce smiles that light up a scene better than any camera flash ever could. The photos that follow feature many dazzling ones, from players, coaches and fans alike, celebrating a goal, a victory or hockey's biggest prize, the Stanley Cup.

While a few of the Stanley Cup champion New York Rangers in a vintage 1928 photo did sport rather serious expressions when they visited Mayor Jimmy Walker, it might have had more to do with respect for the office. As championship shots go, it's certainly the exception rather than the rule. By comparison, witness the expressions of legendary champions like Al Arbour, Mario Lemieux or the young Bobby Orr, work done, arms or Cup aloft.

Off the ice, hockey fans themselves often ride waves of emotion that can last years and even decades. Whether in the stands at the games, at public celebrations or along parade routes, they deserve their moment, too. Some players, in truly classic shots, have remembered to acknowledge that.

The recurring character here, of course, is Lord Stanley's silver cup, the symbol of hockey immortality, players refuse to touch…until they can't keep their hands off it.

Words often fail to properly describe winning. Perhaps these have, too. Photos do a much better job.

Enjoy these winning smiles.

A magnificent moment in Minnesota: Mario Lemieux holds the Stanley Cup aloft in the visitors' dressing room after the Penguins captured the first championship in team history in 1991. Mario "The Magnificent" was awarded the Conn Smythe Trophy as playoff MVP, with 16 goals and 28 assists in 23 playoff games. Despite missing a game in the Final, he finished the series with five goals and seven assists.

Mario Lemieux

HHOF 1997

Met Center · Bloomington , MN | May 25, 1991   Paul Bereswill | colour · slide · 35mm

"There's a hole in my Cup!" No matter, Jean Béliveau had 10 others as a player and seven more as an executive with the Canadiens for 17 total, more than anyone else. As for the hole in the bottom of the Cup? It's now covered by a plate that features the logo of the Hockey Hall of Fame, its official keeper.

Jean Béliveau

HHOF 1972

Twenty-two-year-old Bobby Orr hugs the Cup shortly after scoring the game, series and championship-clincher 40 seconds into overtime in Game 4 of the 1970 Stanley Cup Final. If it seems No. 4 is incredibly young in the photo, consider that NHL teams began scouting him as early as 1960, when he was 12, and the Bruins got his signature on a C-Form committing him to their team two years later. In return for Orr signing, the Bruins gave him $1,000 and committed to a new stucco job on his family home in Parry Sound, Ontario, a used car for his father and a new suit for Bobby himself.

Bobby Orr

HHOF 1979

St. Louis Arena · St. Louis, MO | May 10, 1970 ○ Al Ruelle | B/W · negative · 2¹⁄₄″ x 2¹⁄₄″

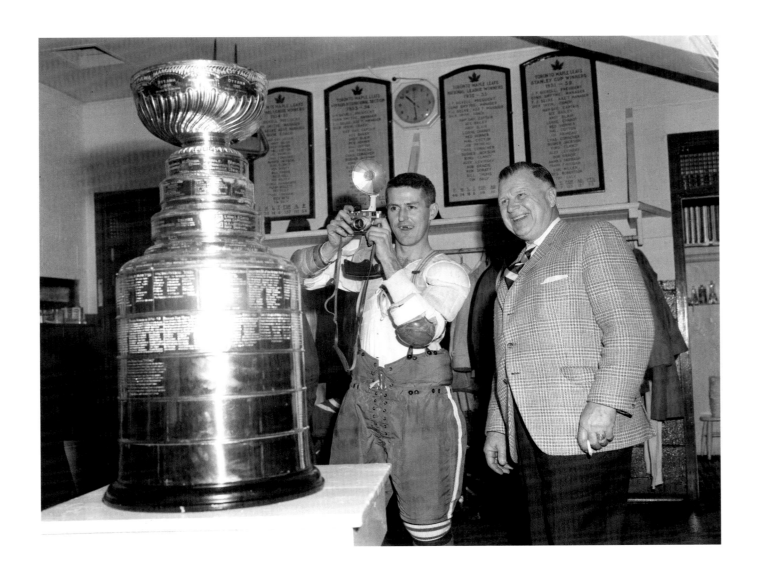

Toronto Maple Leafs winger Billy Harris turns shutterbug alongside team co-owner and Executive Vice-President, Harold Ballard in the Leafs' dressing room after winning the 1963 Stanley Cup. A Toronto native, "Hinky" joined the Leafs in 1956 and helped the team capture three Stanley Cup championships. He was an avid photographer who chronicled his time as a Leaf in *Memoirs of a Decade - 1955-65*.

Billy Harris & Harold Ballard

HHOF 1977

Maple Leaf Gardens · Toronto, ON | April 18, 1963   Graphic Artists | B/W · negative · 4" x 5"

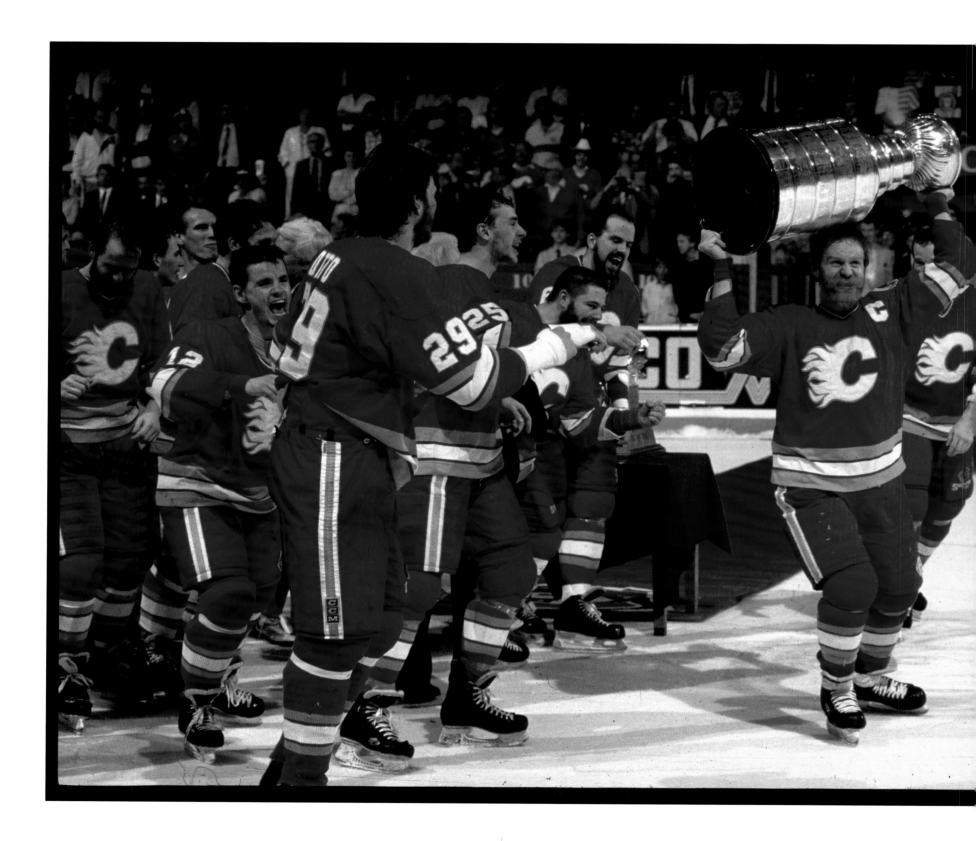

Montreal Forum · Montreal, QC | May 25, 1989 ◯ Paul Bereswill | colour · slide · 35mm

Ending a career on a high note. Calgary Flames' co-captain and current Hockey Hall of Fame Chairman of the Board, Lanny McDonald hoists the Stanley Cup in the Montreal Forum. The 36-year-old McDonald, who had announced that the 1988-89 season would be the last of his 16-year career, scored a second-period goal to give the Flames a 2-1 lead. The game marks the only time the Canadiens lost a Cup-deciding game on home ice.

Lanny McDonald

HHOF 1992

New York Islanders coach Alger "Al" Arbour prepares to take a satisfying drink from the Stanley Cup for the fourth consecutive year. Arbour, who won four championships as a player with Detroit, Chicago and Toronto, helped turn the hapless Islanders around in his second season with the team. He retired from coaching for two years after the 1986 season then returned to lead the Isles for parts of six seasons before retiring in 1994 with 1,499 games under his belt. The Islanders brought him back for one game in 2007, to allow him to reach the 1,500-game milestone.

Al Arbour

HHOF 1996

Nassau Veterans Memorial Coliseum · Uniondale, NY | May 17, 1983 ○ Paul Bereswill | colour · slide · 35mm

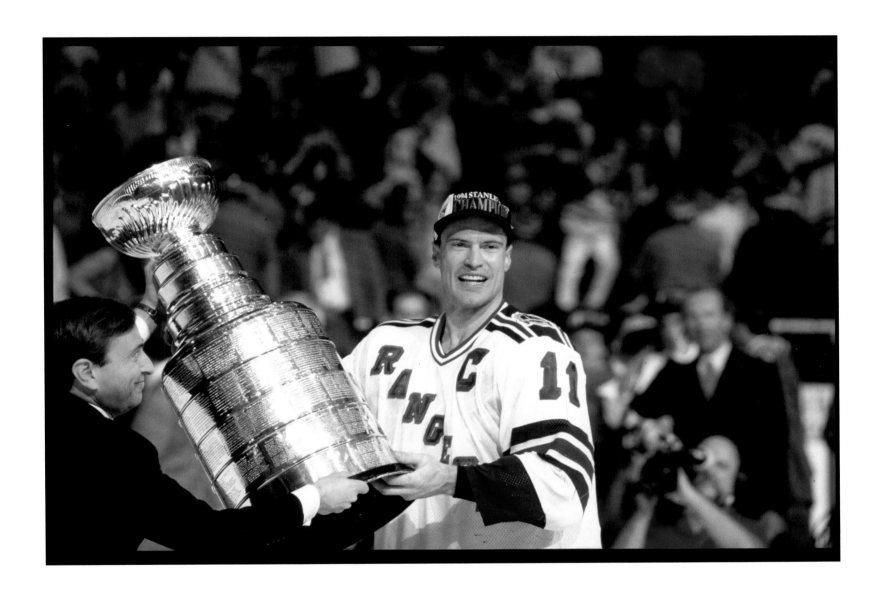

Mark Messier receives the Stanley Cup from Commissioner Gary Bettman after leading the Rangers to their first championship since 1940. The 54-year drought was sometimes called Dutton's Curse, after the NHL and Rangers management angered New York Americans coach and manager Red Dutton, by reneging on a promise to let the Amerks, who suspended operations after the 1942 season, return to Madison Square Garden. Messier won six Stanley Cup championships during his illustrious career.

Mark Messier

HHOF 2007

Madison Square Garden · New York, NY | June 14, 1994   Doug MacLellan | colour · slide · 35mm

Enfin! (finally!). Ray Bourque hoists the Cup after 22 seasons. Bourque's wait for Cup glory was the longest of any player in NHL history, 1,612 regular season and 214 playoff games. After 20 seasons in Boston. the Bruins traded Bourque to Colorado in March 2000 in hopes of seeing him win hockey's most coveted prize, which he eventually did in 2001. Avalanche captain Joe Sakic broke with tradition by letting Bourque have the first skate with the Cup.

Ray Bourque

HHOF 2004

Pepsi Center · Denver, CO | June 9, 2001 Dave Sandford | colour · slide · 35mm

Runneth over for my Cup photo! Photographer access to Stanley Cup presentations these days is limited and controlled. Not so in the early 1980s it would seem, as photographers could chase down players like Islanders defenceman Denis Potvin for a winning shot.

Denis Potvin

HHOF 1991

Nassau Veterans Memorial Coliseum · Uniondale, NY | May 24, 1980 ○ Mecca | colour · slide · 35mm

The 1928 Stanley Cup-winning New York Rangers visit the office of
New York City Mayor, Jimmy Walker. In their second season in the
NHL, the Lester Patrick-led Blueshirts defeated the Montreal Maroons
to become the second American team after the 1917 Seattle Metro-
politans to win the Cup. The Rangers won the best-of-five series 3-2.
With the Ringling Brothers and Barnum & Bailey Circus having taken
over Madison Square Garden, all five games were played on the
Maroons' home ice, the Montreal Forum.

New York Rangers

New York City Hall · New York, NY | April 16, 1928 ◯ Le Studio du Hockey | B/W · glass · 5" x 7"

Basking in the sunshine, and the love of their fans, Serge Savard, Yvan Cournoyer and Michel "Bunny" Larocque of the Montreal Canadiens accompany the Stanley Cup along what would become its "usual route" in 1977 after winning the first of four consecutive championships. An estimated 300,000 people gathered along the parade route to cheer on their passing heroes.

Serge Savard, Yvan Cournoyer & Michel Larocque

HHOF 1986   HHOF 1982

Getting ready for lift-off. Two angles of Bobby Orr's famous flight after his Cup-winner in 1970 capture the Bruins' great a nanosecond after his winner, and just prior to going airborne. St. Louis defenceman Noel Picard and goaltender Glenn Hall were the other principal characters in the play.

Bobby Orr

❧ HHOF 1979 ❧

St. Louis Arena · St. Louis, MO | May 10, 1970 ◯ Lorne Sandler | colour · print · 8" x 10"

CLASSIC PHOTOS

St. Louis Arena · St. Louis, MO | May 10, 1970 ◯ Fred Keenan | B/W · print · 16" x 20"

Phil Esposito is a legend in Boston, where he famously wore the No. 7, the number he sported to start his career in Chicago before the Bruins acquired him in a blockbuster trade in 1967. But when another big trade sent him to New York early in 1976, Esposito faced a dilemma — his trusty number seven was already taken, by Rangers legend Rod Gilbert. Esposito briefly wore the No. 5 before switching to No. 12 for the rest of the 1976-77 season. The following year, he switched to 77. Boston retired No. 7 in Esposito's honour in 1987, with Bruins star Ray Bourque switching to, you guessed it, 77.

Phil Esposito

HHOF 1984

Nassau Veterans Memorial Coliseum · Uniondale, NY | 1975-76   DiMaggio-Kalish | colour · slide · 35mm

"ODD MAN RUSH"

One hundred years of hockey have produced some thrilling moments, but a fair share of quirky ones, too. Some of those captured here are wacky gimmicks dreamed up by a photographer, some are naturally occurring oddities, like a funny expression, and others are rarities that only the keenest of fans might pick up on. For example, find out why Espo (Phil Esposito) wore No. 12, and another number, in the same season.

The "coolest game on earth," to use an old slogan, might just be the fastest, too, so odd things can happen out there on the ice. And so much has changed in the past century that younger fans might be surprised to discover how casually things were done back in the old days, when an opposing player could wander into the photo of a penalty shot instead of being forced to huddle at the bench with the rest of his team.

Indeed, there is plenty here to puzzle the younger fan:

"Dad, why is that referee up there on the boards?"

"Mom, what are all those Maple Leafs doing outside in their uniforms?"

"I thought the Colorado Rockies were a baseball team!"

And then there are the players, like the aforementioned Espo who turns up in a strange jersey after years in another. They say it's the little things that make it all worthwhile. So enjoy these little quirks of hockey, these rarities and oddities.

Fun memories.

Chicago Black Hawks right-winger Bill Mosienko poses with three pucks after scoring the fastest hat trick in NHL history. In the final game of the 1951-52 NHL season, Mosienko scored three goals in a 21-second span against the New York Rangers. The Rangers led the game 6-2 in the third period when "Mosie" scored at 6:09, 6:20 and 6:30. Mosienko narrowly missed a fourth seven seconds later when he hit the post. Chicago scored twice more to win, 7-6.

Bill Mosienko

HHOF 1965

After missing the playoffs in their first full season as the Maple Leafs, Conn Smythe's Toronto hockey squad got down to serious business at their 1928 training camp in Port Elgin, Ontario. The team hired a physical training expert, Corporal Joe Coyne of The Royal Canadian Regiment (in black), to whip the players into shape. Aside from old school calisthenics and running, the training regimen included golf, tennis, softball and fishing. The team got off to an average start, but a strong finish where they lost only three of their final 15 games.

Toronto Maple Leafs

Port Elgin, ON | October 1928 Imperial Oil - Turofsky | B/W · glass · 4" x 5"

Maple Leaf Gardens · Toronto, ON | 1964-65   Harold Barkley | colour · transparency · 2³/₄" x 4¹/₂"

Old Leaf and new Ranger Dick Duff breaks in on Terry Sawchuk, wearing No. 24 for Toronto, in 1964-65, the first season on these teams for each of them. For most of the NHL's first half century, teams carried one goaltender who always wore No. 1. And when a goalie would leave the game with an injury, his replacement, often plucked from the stands, would wear the same number. That created a dilemma in the mid-1960s when the league mandated that teams dress a second netminder. Sawchuk switched to No. 30 the following season, with other goalies following suit.

Terry Sawchuk

HHOF 1971

Boston defenceman Johnny "Jack" Crawford, with Toronto's Don Metz, was one of the first NHLers to wear a helmet. In fact, a number of Bruins were among hockey's early helmeted players. The very first may have been George Owen, who wore his Harvard football helmet during the 1928-29 season. In Crawford's case, the leather helmet wasn't entirely for better protection, but rather to cover his bald head.

Johnny Crawford

Maple Leaf Gardens · Toronto, ON | 1948-49 ⌀ Imperial Oil-Turofsky | B/W · negative · 4" x 5"

Referee Frank Udvari scales the glass to make way for Montreal defenceman J.C. Tremblay, as goaltender Jacques Plante follows the play. The colourful Udvari often perched upon the dasher to avoid interfering with the play. Retired from on-ice officiating since 1966, Udvari laced them up a final time, at the age of 54, on December 30, 1978, after referee Dave Newell suffered an injury.

Frank Udvari

HHOF 1973

A trick of the light, or perspective, perhaps. Thomas Vanek
of the Buffalo Sabres appears to get a mouthful of Ottawa
Senators defenceman Sergei Gonchar's stick in this 2011
game. Enquiring minds want to know…if that referee raised
his arm to signal a high-sticking penalty moments later.

Thomas Vanek

Seventeen years before there was a baseball team of the same name, and 19 years before the Quebec Nordiques moved to Denver to become the Colorado Avalanche, the Colorado Rockies made their NHL debut. Born from the ashes of the short-lived Kansas City Scouts, the Rockies struggled for most of their six-year existence. NHL notables who suited up for the Rockies include Lanny McDonald, acquired from Toronto, Joel Quenneville, goaltender Glenn "Chico" Resch and Rob Ramage, the first overall choice in the 1979 NHL Entry Draft. The team became the New Jersey Devils in 1982.

Colorado Rockies

St. Louis Arena · St. Louis, MO | December 10, 1977 ○ Portnoy | colour · slide · 35mm

Northwestern High School Outdoor Rink · Detroit, MI | 1927-28 ◯ Le Studio du Hockey | B/W · glass · 5" x 7"

George Hay of the Detroit Cougars is shown during an outdoor prac-
tice in the 1927-28 season. The Cougars, who joined the NHL in 1926,
became the Detroit Falcons in 1930 and the Red Wings in 1932, may
have occasionally scrimmaged outdoors that year. With 22 goals
and 13 assists, Hay was the team's top point-getter that season. An
expert stickhandler, he earned the nickname "The Western Wizard"
for playing in the Western Canada Hockey League.

George Hay

HHOF 1958

Simpler times. In today's NHL, for many years, in fact, players from both teams must remain on their respective benches while a penalty shot is taken. Here, an unknown New York Rangers player has a much better view as he, linesman George Hayes and referee Bill Chadwick watch Tod Sloan of the Toronto Maple Leafs bear down on Rangers goalie Chuck Rayner. Rayner made the save and New York won the game, 2-0.

Tod Sloan

Maple Leaf Gardens · Toronto, ON | February 17, 1951   Imperial Oil - Turofsky | B/W · negative · 4" x 5"

Man down! Chicago Black Hawks goaltender Mike Karakas cranes his neck for a better view while his teammate, Earl Seibert, and Gord Drillon of the Toronto Leafs battle for position in front of him during the 1938-39 season. Meanwhile, another Toronto player has fallen…and can't get up, in the corner. The same two teams had faced each in the previous season's Stanley Cup Final, with Chicago capturing the second championship in its history.

Black Hawks vs Leafs

Chicago Stadium · Chicago, IL | 1938-39   Le Studio du Hockey | B/W · negative · 4" x 5"

This intriguing portrait of Reginald "Red" Horner was taken no later than the 1931-32 season, depicting the palpable intensity of the tough-as-nails Leafs defenceman. Horner would help the Leafs to their third franchise Cup in 1932 and become team captain in 1938, but is perhaps best remembered for his willingness to drop his heavy leather gauntlets. Upon his retirement in 1940, Horner was the NHL's all-time leader in penalty minutes with 1,254.

Red Horner

HHOF 1965

Location Unknown | c.1931-32 ⏀ Imperial Oil-Turofsky | B/W · glass · 4" X 5"

CLASSIC PHOTOS

These photos capture Bill Barilko's famous goal that night in Toronto, culminating in a classic Stanley Cup-winning smile from the lost hero. As hockey legends go, few match the intrigue and tragedy of the Barilko story. As told, re-told and sung, his overtime winner won the Leafs the Cup in 1951. He was lost in a plane crash that summer, only to have his body recovered from the wreckage 11 years later, the year of the Leafs' next Cup win.

Bill Barilko

Maple Leaf Gardens · Toronto, ON | April 21, 1951 ⊕ Hockey Hall of Fame | B/W · copy negative · 4" x 5"

Maple Leaf Gardens · Toronto, ON | April 21, 1951 ⏀ Michael Burns Sr. | B/W · negative · 4" x 5"

Maple Leaf Gardens · Toronto, ON | April 21, 1951 ⬦ Michael Burns Sr. | B/W · negative · 4" x 5"

A heartfelt 'thank you' to the fantastic team of people who worked together to make this book the best it could be.

Here's the lineup:

Our partner, the Hockey Hall of Fame, and its amazing team, including Phil Pritchard, Craig Campbell, Steve Poirier, Peter Jagla and Courtney Evans.

Salma Belhaffaf, for your beautiful vision of this book.

Judy Yelon, for your eagle eye; Anne Nice, for your editing; and Isabelle Delage, for your elegant French translation and proofreading.

Debby deGroot, for helping us make sure everyone knows about this book!

Rob Dawson, for your patience, guidance and support throughout this process.

Our printing partner Friesens, for helping us reproduce these incredible photos with such richness. To AMP, for additional shipping and handling support.

Benito Aloe, for your sage counsel and hockey anecdotes.

Members of the Taddeo Monday Night Hockey League, for market research and refreshments!

Finally, thank you to all the hockey fans who love sharing memories!